It Crescendos

It Crescendos

A Poetry Collection
The Oklahoma years

VOLUME ONE

Delon Nicole Starkey

FIRST EDITION

Cover Art by Anthony Coursey
Illustrations by Anthony Coursey
Cover and Interior Design by Bret Brewer

ISBN 979-8-218-03359-0 (paperback)

To my Nana:

The inspiration behind it all. You were a writer and a dreamer and my lifelong cheerleader. Your words kept me going when mine kept me from moving forward.

To my Family & Friends:
Mom and Dad—for always believing that I could.
Hubby—for pushing me forward on the days I wanted to move backward.
Kiddos—You're never too young or old to accomplish your dreams. I hope you always find the light and desire to follow yours.

Friends & Everyone Else:
Thanks for believing in me and supporting me in this crazy and wonderful adventure. I owe you one!

Contents

Foreword
Introduction

1. Crescendo
2. A Cappella
3. Ballad
4. Melody
5. Harmony

FOREWORD

When Delon asked if I would write the foreword for her book, I was tremendously honored and super excited! Seeing her write this book has been an incredible journey, and it is quite difficult to capture just how incredible in only a few short paragraphs. But I'll try and paint the picture for you. This book is not a year or two or even five in the making. This book is over a decade and a half in the making!

Delon and I are one of those crazy couples that met online through eHarmony.com (go ahead, you can cheer for us if you want!). We first started talking and met in the summer of 2015. And I'm almost positive it was one of the very first times we met that she showed me some of her poetry. She said she'd been writing poetry for as long as she could remember.

She showed me some folder on her old MacBook (that took forever to boot up mind you and I was terrified at the thought of it crashing), and she told me that one day she'd like to somehow publish a book of her poems. Remember, this is 2015.

Poetry pours out of Delon. She would continue to write and share her poetry with me here and there throughout our entire time together. As the saying goes though, that funny thing called Life happens, and months and years begin to slip by like you're hurtling down the freeway. We got married in 2016, had our daughter in 2017, Delon stayed at home with her for a couple of years, then went back to work part time, we had our son in 2021... and still no poetry book. Sometimes it seemed like a distant memory of a dream, sometimes it would briefly bubble up to the surface, only to go back down again amidst Cheerios and boogers and dirty laundry.

Then 2022 came and somehow something changed. Some spark hit her in a way it never had before. It wasn't just a momentary flicker that disappeared as quickly as it came. It was like that spark was hitting an enormous pile of wood that was beyond ready to burn. It wanted to burn. It needed to burn. And burn it did! Delon began working at a feverish pace toward her goal. Compiling her poems from bunches of random places, printing them, formatting them, temporarily storing them in a binder, editing them, researching publishing options, etc. etc...

And now here we are. Here YOU are. Holding this book. A real book. For real life. You did it babe!! I am so so proud of you. I believed in you--- I knew you could do it; I love you so much! And you, *dear reader*, are in for a treat. This book was a long time coming, and I think you'll be as glad as me that she finally did it. The crescendo begins!

Philip W. Starkey, *forevermate*

INTRODUCTION

You know when you've been telling yourself you're going to do something for years and years but then nothing actually happens? And then one day you wake up and you just *do it*? Yes, that's exactly what happened.

I was walking through the aisles at Walmart. Pretty basic right? It wasn't even an aisle I needed to go down (guilty!) but something compelled me to walk down that aisle anyway. Next thing I know, I found myself standing in the book aisle. So, here's where the magic started to happen. I picked up what I thought was just an ordinary, run-of-the-mill, average Joe book, but to my surprise, it was a *poetry* book. Might seem mundane or boring to you, but it was just the push of inspiration I needed to **dive** right in.

That's usually where the story ends for me, the spark burns quickly but then fizzles out. The funny part is I didn't even buy the book that day. I came back on a different day and bought the book after starting the tedious process of what it might look like to publish a book myself. But for whatever reason, that day, that moment, that book, was the final straw that yelled, *Wake up, and write this dang book already!* And so, as you can see, I did a thing. Now let me tell you a little more about this *thing*.

It Crescendos is a collection of poetry written from the heart over the span of the last 20 years. I have written poetry, along with short stories and lyrics and journals, for as long as I can remember. Writing is in my blood. It's a huge part of what makes me who I am. Writing for me is a lifeline, a safe place to escape to, and the most vulnerable and honest way I know how to fully express myself.

The beginning of this poetry collection takes place during a time that I felt most vulnerable and exposed. I am calling this The Oklahoma Years because truly, that's where it all began. Here in the heart of Oklahoma. We moved from Plano, TX to northwest Oklahoma around the time I was thirteen. And if you know, then you know just how difficult life can be at thirteen.

At the time, it was by far the biggest transition I'd ever been through, and it hit me hard to say the least. It felt like starting over. I essentially was writing a new chapter in my story, and it wasn't one I was ready to write at that age. But writing I did, nonetheless. Honestly, I'm not sure I would be writing to you right now if I somehow weren't able to express all my deepest and darkest thoughts on paper. I found myself writing constantly and it was my safest place that I could truly be <u>free</u>.

Introduction

I wrote when I was angry. I wrote when I felt sad, or unsure of myself (which was quite often), or when I thought I was in love, or when I experienced heartbreak... I wrote it all down. I didn't miss a single moment or emotion. I hope that as you read this collection you will be able to *freely* experience some of these same colors of emotions that I was trying to get across the page. But more importantly, I hope that it means something special to you. Whether or not it relates directly to you, I hope it tells a story that you can imagine yourself being a part of and that you can somehow make fit into your own journey no matter where you may be right now.

I hope this collection can relate to you in the hard times, but also be a light to you and inspire you and encourage you to keep on keeping on. We all have a voice and although these are simply words on a page, it is my sincere hope that somehow, they might mean a little something more.

I wrote these at times when I felt that my voice was small, and I did not feel heard. Either by the world or my family or even myself, and God. But in the midst of all of this, somewhere along the journey I found hope again. I found a light within, and my soul was re-lit with a flame that would not burn out. It started out with a slow, quiet tempo, but gradually the sound began to increase. I could feel it in my very bones growing louder and louder and louder until it echoed all around me. My voice crescendoed off the pages, my words were suddenly a vibrant blaze, and I knew at that moment that I would never allow myself to feel silenced ever again.

This is for you readers, and it is my honest hope and prayer, that you too will speak loudly and boldly and that your words will not go unheard.

All my love,

Crescendo

(kreh-SHEN-doh)

TO GRADUALLY GROW LOUDER

It Crescendos

It crescendos
I don't know where it comes from
This slow build inside
Wait for the avalanche to collide.

Crumbling down
Like crumbs off a toddler's chin
Small knee scrapes
From falling off a bike.

The quick rise
Of an ocean tide
A swarm of bees
Surrounding their hive.

Time flies by
Like the whoosh of an airplane
A swimmer taking a dive
Heading for the deep.

It crescendos
Whispering softly and then YELLING
Like the roar of a lion
At the top of his lungs!

Like a small seed
Sprouting tiny leaves

Until one day it's an evergreen
Vibrant and bursting
Dancing in the breeze.

A young girl
Trembling in her shoes
Too shy to meet an eye
She goes unnoticed.

A teenage dream
Lost in a fantasy
Boys and girls
Hopeless heartbreak.

Young adult
Let us begin again
Explore the world
See what I can do.

Mom of two
Married a goof
But finally fits in her shoes
The time to begin is now.
It's rising up
From somewhere inside
Somehow, it had been there all along
No turning back now.
She may be a slow riser
But she's a fast learner

Determined more than ever
Her sights are set.

The music is growing louder
The walls are beginning to shake
The earth is moving
The ground is breaking
Something amazing is about to happen.

Do you feel it?
Can you hear it?

Hands are clapping
People are shouting
Her voice isn't a whisper anymore
She prepares for the encore.
Feet are stomping
Fists are pumping
The words are coming to life!

Shoes are tapping
Fingers are snapping
Her words are becoming stronger
Hearts are pounding
The rhythm is moving!
Do you feel it?
Can you hear it?
Her words will never be silenced
The pen is her sword

Fear will not overcome her
It is time to win this war!

Her life will not be a *shadow*
Creeping on the walls
But a legacy to follow
In the rest of her tomorrows.

Her actions are **loud**
But her words shout **LOUDER**
It crescendos all around her
Like the crashing sound of cymbals
Nothing now can stop her.

She will never stop the pen from writing
Never delay her fingers from typing
Because it's who she's always been and always will be.

New Beginnings

New beginnings surround me
I have been awakened--- asleep for too long
Today the sun shines
And the clouds have found somebody else to shade.

Like a flower, I bloom
Warm, like late June
If ice cubes were to touch my skin, they would melt.
Tiny raindrops on the glass---shimmering, sparkling.

I do not evaporate in the light; I am reaching out
Glowing in this new sunlight
And happy because I am found.

Just a Dream

Thunder rolls and I am awake
I'm alive but I'm still dreaming
Rain pounds tiny fists against my windowpane.
Here I find myself once again,
Vulnerable and exposed---everything shows.
I cannot hide here when the rain whispers *go!*
Soft voices vibrate against the glass
Against the gloom that fills this room
Then I flip on the switch, and on comes the light.
My entire being awakened, brought back to life!
I open my eyes and realize that it was all just a dream.
Soon after I find myself drifting back to sleep,
With the comfort in knowing that I will be alright.

For My Dad

Every year it gets harder and harder
To figure out what everybody wants
Whether it's birthday, or Christmas, or just because---
You are the hardest to gift.
Please and thank you's
And I love you's
Tickle fights and Guitar Hero
You have always been my true Hero.

You are stern, but mean well
You set the bar high, and I do my best to reach it
You are a leader, and I am a follower
I have always looked up to you
You have set a great example
And I try to be more like you.

Nothing could replace you
No one could love like you do
Your love is unconditional and so is mine for you
You hold our family together
You and mom are the glue
Looking back, at what we have,
I could not have asked for a greater Dad.

IT CRESCENDOS

I am still learning from you every day
All the things I should or shouldn't say
How to love and how to forgive
And all the second chances I need to give.

I learned how to trust
And to take a leap of faith
How to stand firm
And not back down
Dad, you have shown me who I am.

Without you, I would not be the same
Without you, life would be empty
Because you have given me so much
More than words can describe.

Because of you, I am not afraid to speak my heart,
Because of you, I have the courage to start,
Because of you, I am who I am,
But most of all I am thankful for you, Dad.

For My Mom

Another year has come and gone,
It was hardly even noticed.
Without you, we would all be a mess
A permanent space inside my chest.

Life is fast and often unexpected
When the wind blows and the hurricane hits
Lost in the dark, stepping on shadows
Yet somehow your little light always shone bright.

I am sorry for what the storm
Has done to your ship
If you don't know, then you don't know
Because you have never walked with a chip.

You fought the battle
And won in the end
Disease did not overwhelm you
When it should have pulled you in.

I saw you as a warrior
You did not give in to defeat
Faith in your Savior
You could not see.

I grew closer to you that day
Fear and regret pushed away
Left behind with all the things
I never had the courage to say.

You are the soul that radiates
My shining armor in the form of
light
You have loved me all these years
And through my darkest nights.

You didn't hate me in the valley
When I was at my lowest of lows
You shouted your love from the rooftops
That reached me down below.

I cannot describe how much you mean
There are no words that could compare
To whom you are and all that you do
I love the amazing person you are.

I thank God that you are my mom
And I thank Him for gifting me to you
A bond so strong it will never crack
Mom, I love you to the moon and back.

Crescendo

Powerless Words That Have the Spark to Ignite

I can no longer dream
That you're here with me
I cannot convince myself that you are
When I know you clearly are not.

I can no longer pretend
That you're protecting me from harm
Because when you're not around
Waves of insecurity rush back in.

There are nights I cannot stop the tears
Worry creeps in that you will disappear
I am in my bed all alone
But I do not bother picking up my phone.

Wishing you were here
Love, you are not forgotten
You arc impossible to forget
But impossible to be without.

My heart knows it is time to say goodbye
So, to you I will write these final words
I will kill the space with meaningful lines
Of powerless words that have the spark to ignite.

Things I Never Said

What if you knew the way I felt?
About you...
Would it freak you out?
Or would it blow your mind away?

I wish you could see my smile
Sometimes I cry when I think about
The times I needed someone
And you were always right there.

You would look at me crazy
If I said this aloud
That's why I'm sending you a message in a bottle,
signed, *True love waiting*.

Sometimes I question if I am making a mistake
What we have is special
And I believe in our friendship
But what if that is all we will ever be?

Among all my distractions
I'd have to say you're the best
So much for sappy "love songs"
This will be the ultimate test.

If only I had the courage to say
All the words floating in my head
That keep going and going and going.
But for now, I will keep this
In a separate stack, saved for later.

Out of sight, out of mind
Along with all the things I... oh, never mind.

Hilltop Bruises

I've got hilltop bruises
And a million scars
Chase me down
With your fancy cars.
I'm getting by just fine
I've made it through today,
And it's all good.

I've got dirty dishes in the sink
Yesterday's clothes
Spread out on the floor
Yesterday's notes
I've been trying to keep it straight
I can't keep up
With this place anymore
But I will not complain,
I am not that vain.

I've got hilltop bruises
And valley excuses
I can't keep up with my chores
Or half of my world.
The waits-last-minute
Try-and-fix-it-up-quick kind of girl.
Skinned knees
I like to play rough
Until words cut like knives

Do not tell me what I am
Because I know that I'm enough
I can be brave
I have the nerve
To embrace the fall because I will.

I'm too much for this city
I'm feeling homesick
This wasn't the card
I wanted to lay down
I'm a weed in the wind
My hair all tangled up
I don't know where I am going
But I won't be giving up.

I have made it through today
And so far, that's OK.

While I Wait

Be still came the whisper from within
Breathe in this moment, it may never come again.
It is so hard sometimes, with life rushing by
To let go and allow things to be the way they come.

We live in the now, always wanting things to happen
immediately.
Be still is the last thing we want to hear.
But when we finally settle, we begin to open our eyes.
We start to see things we have not seen before.

They say, *For every closed door, a new one opens.*
I wanted to believe that, but I did not want to wait.
All my life I have been told that,
Everything happens for a reason
Easy to say when you are not handed all the reasons.

I waited and watched as the seasons passed through;
another love that came and went like summer through
winter.
Every stranger that would catch my eye
I could not help but question, "Is this person mine?"
I would not hear a single word, not a hint, a dream, or
anything.

Be still returned the persistent whisper
At one point I started to cry
Because I did not understand.
What was I really waiting for,
How long was I supposed to wait?
That is when I fell to my knees, demanding to know
Why this part was so hard for me.

I felt the presence of God
I could hear His voice.
He said *Child of mine, why is your head so low?*
Don't you know that I have great plans for you?
I know your deepest desires,
I've heard the broken cries from your heart.
If only you could see what I see,
Then would you see the bigger part?

I make you wait not to make you hurt,
But to prepare you for what I have in store.
I want your heart to be whole in me,
Not just for anybody—for all you ever need is me.

So, I decided I would wait,
No matter how long or little it would take
To find the one God's promised to me.
And in the meantime, I will choose to be happy
Happy while I wait.

Chocolate Milk

He is beautiful when he sleeps
The way he smiles and kicks when he dreams.
Then I reach over to tickle him, and he screams
I'm so in love with him.

When I wake up his arm will be around me
The alarm is going off, it's five-thirty
But he's trying to hurry me out the door
So, I'm not late for work again...oh man, I love him.

He asks me a silly thing before I go...

"Can you make me some chocolate milk?"
I look at him like he's crazy
I don't know what makes him think of these things,
Even though I'm running late
I open the fridge and grab the milk
He tells me I had better stir it good
Because he likes it to taste smooth
And I can tell he's not in the mood for an attitude.

I simply do my best
Trying not to spill and make a giant mess
Yeah, I really love him
Even when he doesn't make sense.
I'll love him for the rest of our days
Even though he loves chocolate milk.

When I get home from work
I can smell supper cooking
It's been another exhausting day
And I'm beat.

He smiles at me and kisses me on the lips
I ask him what he's making
But he just laughs and says,
"You'll find out!"

We're getting ready to wrap up the night
I climb into bed and turn out the lights
He looks up at me, with those innocent eyes
And it's almost as if he sings to me,

"Hey babe, can you make me some chocolate milk?"
I just look at him like he's crazy
Because maybe he is a little *(don't tell him that)*
I smile and nod, and reply, "Sure thing"
Even though I'm exhausted
 I would rather be by his side.

He reminds me I'd better mix it up good
Because he can't stand the chunks of chocolate
Coating up the sides.
I'm trying to do my best not to spill and make a mess
Man, I love him,
But sometimes he doesn't make sense.
I love him anyway, and he loves chocolate milk.

He is beautiful when he sleeps
The way he smiles and kicks when he dreams.
How I love to tickle him
When he giggles and lets out a tiny scream.
I love him for always,
Especially on the days
He asks me to make him some chocolate milk.

Restart Button

Shut me out, I walk on my own
Please, just leave me alone
I don't need your lies so take them away
You promise me one thing, but it's different every day.

Hope is forgotten as the silence becomes our sound.
We no longer have a connection, lost but never found.
Do I even cross your thoughts at all?
Would you be there to catch my fall?

Our hearts are bleeding black and blue
I am giving up on trying to save you
There is only pain piercing my heart
I am sick of running; I wish we could restart.

I tremble from fear that grips me tight
There's a leak in our boat, I am not alright
Nowhere to go, no place I can hide
Like a rose without water
I withered and died.

Love didn't want me, it didn't understand
I will push you away if you reach for my hand.
I am letting go of this love I once knew
Things would be better if I hadn't met you.

Phoebe

Outside there was a clatter
Pitter patter, pitter patter
One would ask her, *Phoebe what's the matter?*
But she never answered her telephone,
Outside there is a clatter.

The windows too tall, she climbs a ladder
She watches the rain fall, inside a world of her own.
Pitter patter, pitter patter.

Childhood memories
She's feeling sadder
For the mistakes she's made
If only she had known...
Outside there is clatter.

Teardrops on the windowpane
Splatter, frozen in memory
Solid like a stone
Pitter patter, pitter patter.

Thunder strikes
Her thoughts stagger
Shivers run up and down her spine
Outside there is a clatter
Pitter patter, pitter patter.

Forevermore

Ask the questions
I'll have the answers
Even if it takes up all my time
I'll sing the songs
I'll read the rhymes
And hold you near because you're mine.

I am a tower
That I'll let you climb
There are no secrets
I'll always let you in
I'll laugh at your jokes
Memorize all your little pokes
Because your fingers still fit in mine.

Build the forts
And tear them down
Be a lion
Be a princess
Be anything you want.
Imagination is precious
But tomorrow is fleeting
You, my DARLING, are not.

I'll watch your favorite movies
One hundred times over
We'll memorize all the lines
Make the make-believe come alive
Because when I'm with you
My inner child comes to life.

I love you today
Yesterday and tomorrow
You are wrapped up tight
Snug around my heart
And I just play the part.

I am your mother
I'll be your best friend
I'm your defender until the end
I'm your cheerleader
You're boldest fighter
Educator and provider.

I don't quit on the hard days
And believe me those do come
But my love for you is forever
It's unconditional.

There's nothing you will ever do
That will make me love you less
You're the reason for my tears
But also, for my joy and happiness.

I am proud
I am stronger
I am bolder because of you
I am wiser
I am learning all the time
I am blessed beyond all measure
To forever call you mine.

You're bound to me
Woven in the womb
This is a love made just for you
Can't be bought or found anywhere else
Delicately handcrafted just to you.

I am Mama
I am Mom
I am Yours
You are Daughter
You are Son
And I'll love you both forevermore.

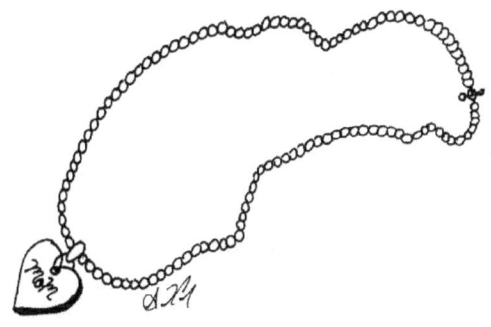

Happily, Ever After, It's Not the End

Growing up I believed in fairytales
Where the princes met the princesses
They fell in love
Happily, ever after, the end.

The first boy that came along
I told myself that he could be the one
I gave away my heart
But he tore it apart.

I tried to pick up the pieces
But I was picking up glass
The more I tried to fix it
The deeper I fell into the past.

I finally was able to walk away from it all
Promised myself that never again would I fall
For anyone, for as long as I lived.

Then another came along
He hummed a different song
A song so beautiful that it captured me.

Away with him, he set my heart free
Light as a feather like the wings of an angel
He carried me, carried me away.

Crescendo

When I found him, I found myself
Packed up the old me and became someone else
I am who I want to be, and I am happy
Happily, ever after, it's not the end.

I waited patiently for this day to come
When you found yourself on one knee
Asking me to be your bride, little ole me
We were as light as feathers like the wings of an angel,
And you carried us away, carried us away.

When I found you, I found myself
Left the old me behind and became someone else
I am who I want to be,
Never knew I could be this happy,
Until the day I met you.

Happily, ever after, it's not the end
This chapter isn't closing: this is where it all begins.

The TV

Raindrops
Pelting on the rooftops
Above me
I can hear it
Softly as it sings to me
Raindrops
How I wish they would
Dance through the glass
If only they could save me
From my lonely misery
Wash me away
Raindrops.

Crackling
The mighty sound of thunder
Vibrating these four walls
I am sinking in my chair
The fabric glues me in
Crackling
Like tiny pieces breaking
Longing for escape now
From these four walls
Caging me in
The raging storm outside.

Fogging
Up the windows
I gently press my breath upon them
It is somehow soothing yet forgettable
Fogging
I trace tiny circles in the mist
Figure eights and loop-the-loops
Sometimes I feel my brain is a circus
Clown faces and balloon animals
Laugh with the rhythm of the rain.

Windows
Pounding tiny fistfuls of hail
The sky blackens
Into a sea of midnight
A dark wedding veil
Curious, but cautious
I stare out the window
But it's impossible to see past
The haunting echo of my reflection.

Crouching
Inside my closet
Lights are out
The house is silent
Radio static
Nothing is coming through
Eyes closed
Pillow hugged tight against my chest

Crouching
Trying to cancel out the fear
That is found in the floor here.

Crashing
The walls cave in around me
I am the eye of the storm
Safety
I long to be
When something suddenly
Comes to me
Alone in this house
Eyes shut tight
Willing the courage
To make sure everything is all right.

Sunrise
Morning comes
Unapologetically bright
I wipe the fog from my eyes
Preparing for the worst
But I am shocked to see
What is in front of me
Nothing but a small black TV
No trace of rain
No hint of a storm
Just the chaos left in my brain.

My Reflection

Sometimes I reflect a *cloudy gray*
Gloomy, wide-eyed, cautious, and awake
Then there are days I'm a glowing green—
Jealous, full of envy.
Other days I'm yellows and pinks, orange too
Happy and
      ~   c a r e f r e e   ~
Bubbly and vibrant
I'm a pool of many colors
But all of these are tiny reflections of me.

Love You So

It kills me that you're leaving, love
But I know that you must go
I cannot face the truth
It's hitting me hard
I'm down to the last card
I cannot keep playing your games
I know that it's time for you to go
But there's something I want you to know.

When you walk away love,
It's going to break my heart
Even though we will be apart
I hope you'll think of me
Every time you close your eyes.
Do you think of me?
Does your heart hurt when you're alone?

I hope that one day you will find real love
A love I wish were still mine
I hope you love her better
And give her all your time
It breaks me a little to think of you this way
But it wasn't meant to be for us, love
I wish there were another way.

It kills me to see you go, love
But I know we won't forget
Those long nights together we spent
Staying up late just talking
About whatever came to mind.

We could have stayed that way forever
Forget about the time
The time you lost your way
And said words you should never say
Now I really must say goodbye
Time to dry my eyes
Love, I really must go
But know that I love you so.

Blue Jeans

He's got the ripped jeans
I've been here before
Can't help it, I'm staring
Leaves me wanting more.

Mind made up, I've locked the door
I tell myself he's the one
And ask myself
What am I still looking for?

He's just like the rest
Another boy that's snagged my interest
Blue jeans torn in the seams
The blue is starting to fade
Look at the mess we've made.

He's got that crooked smile I adore
Hand in his pockets as he walks out the door
Can't help it, I'm staring
Leaves me wanting more.

Mind made up, but I've been here before
When will I wake up and realize,
That we are snagged in all the lies?
But then I find you in my bed
And you know how to get inside my head.

Crescendo

I've got to shake my head out of this mess
Throw away all the doubts and regrets
I can't keep you a secret
The perfume of you lingers like cigarettes.

Mind made up, I've been here before
Blue jeans on I'm heading out the door
You're like an old pair, fading
Crumpled on the floor.
Goodbye Blue Jeans, I don't need you anymore

Our Sky is Everybody's Sky

Have you ever wondered
Why the sun shines so bright?
Have you ever thought about the fact that
Our sky is everybody's sky?
When the rain falls
It'll wash away your tears
Have no fear, God is here
Our sky is everybody's sky.
Hear the angel's voices echo
Trembling through the clouds
So close they can touch Jesus
And never wonder why.
Why the bird sings his song
And why memories fade away
Why when we wake it's a new day
And when we close our eyes, it is night.
God knows me better than I do
He can sing me every lullaby
He can hear every heartbreaking cry
And will be there to dry every eye.
Because our sky is everybody's sky.

Nothing

Nothing is ever what it seems
Nothing is ever like our dreams
Nothing is ever as simple as they make it
Nothing is ever easy unless you fake it.

Happy Birthday

Red and gold ribbons in her hair
Today is her birthday and her parents aren't there.
But she's too busy with the presents to care.
Today she turns five.

Jamie and her dad go fishing by the lake
They don't catch anything for the hour's too late.
Too busy to notice that her dad has forgotten.
Today she turns nine.

A brand-new paint gun in his hands
Today is his birthday and his parents have plans.
But he's too busy with friends to care.
Today he turns thirteen.

Now all of them grown into adults
In a world full of busy and too many distractions
To notice that today is indeed their birthday
Because today is just another day, they turn old.

Blue Skies

There are times I don't want to wake up
I'd rather lie in my bed
There are times I want to give up
I can't rid these thoughts from my head.

I open the window
Lift my head to the sky
I see nothing but---

Blue skies
Telling me everything will be all right
Blue skies
To get me through another night
Blue skies
Remind me that life can be beautiful
Even when I cannot see the blue.

There are nights I cannot sleep
I toss and turn but will not dream
There are nights that I pray
Hoping for a new day.

The Lord hears my cries
He never leaves my side
When I wake
I am reminded of His grace, with these

IT CRESCENDOS

Blue skies
Telling me everything will be all right
Blue skies
To get me through another night
Blue skies
Remind me that life can be beautiful
Even when I cannot see the blue.

Sometimes you are going to hurt
Sometimes you are going to cry
Someone's going to break your heart
Loved ones are going to die
You are going to make mistakes
Time and time again
But God keeps his promises
To love and love again, by sending us---

Blue skies
Everything will be all right
Blue skies
You can make it another night
Blue skies
To remind you life can be beautiful
Even when you cannot see the blue.

Amazing

When I look at you, I can't help but smile
Your warm embrace, can you stay awhile?
Safe in your arms I have found a place
Bound by faith and His amazing grace.

You have shown me what it is to love
And you have brought me to the Father above
I couldn't ask for anyone else
You're amazing, truly amazing.

Can you please stay a little while?
Hold on dear, it doesn't stop here
Can you please stay right here?
I'm not going anywhere.

Your laughter is like a fire that burns in my heart
You're the light in the dark when I can't find my way
You're the face of hope I needed
When I was at the end of my rope.

Your joy brings me peace when I cannot cope
Your love burns brighter than the sun,
Don't you ever let go
There's something you should always know
You're amazing, truly amazing.

IT CRESCENDOS

There have been times in my life
Where nothing was clear
Lost inside myself, trapped inside fear
But I didn't let go to the things I know.

I asked God to lead me
I asked Him to guide my feet
He lifted me up and carried me
So don't you let go, keep holding on.

Can you please stay a little while?
Hold on dear it doesn't end here
Can you please stay a little while?
He's not going anywhere
And neither am I.

He'll wrap you in His arms
Hold you tight
He'll wipe your tears
And get you through another night
Nothing is ever what it seems
He wants you to know a simple thing

You're amazing, truly amazing.

A Cappella

(ah kahp-PEL-lah)

MUSIC PERFORMED WITHOUT ACCOMPANIMENT OF INSTRUMENTS

Before the Storm

The waves were calm before the storm
Hidden behind shadows from the sun
Light shone through tiny windows
The day may be done but night had just begun.

That's when the rain began to pour
A shiny silver bullet inside a gun
Dainty dents along the sand
In the corner where the lighthouse met the land.

Red, white, and blue were its colors
Home of the free
White sea foam arms reaching
Out of the sea.

Lost ships were often drawn to her
As she called them back to shore
Guiding sailors with her light
Rescuing them once more.

She rarely received thanks
Certainly not a praise
With every passing day
Waiting for the next one to save.

She was quiet and still as the seagull
Hunting for his prey
Watching over her people
Protecting them night and day.

On this day, the weather was different
And she couldn't figure out why
Until she noticed the little boat
Desperate to stay afloat.

She beamed her light from every direction
For if she had a voice she would shout
Every life is worth saving
That she had no doubt.

Ka-Boom

I am a song
Makes you want to sing along
When it comes on you can't turn away
A song about sorrow and pain
About regret and tears in the rain
I am the kind of song
You can't help but to hum along.

I am bird
Flying south for the winter
The winds are cold, but it is time to go
Away, away, I'll return someday
A bird on a journey
We'll see where it leads me
Or will my wings break
And I take a great fall?
Down on the pavement
With a final ka-boom.

Just Us Kids

Can we go back to '05?
Chalk drawings on the sidewalk
First time love makes you come alive
Words stick like bubble gum
Late nights meant dirt roads
Singing out loud like you don't care
Life's too short to worry about what's fair
Wind in your air, hand in the air
Heart still young, soul set free
Because we aren't yet 18
Young and dumb, that's all you see
But I don't see it that way at all
When I carved our names into the wall
Like Humpty Dumpty we took a great fall
But just us kids, we had it all.

Brave *(For Conner)*

You were braver than me
When you pulled that trigger
With your last breath
Saying goodbye to tomorrow and yesterday.

Bullet to your head
No second thoughts
The next second you were gone
No turning back.

You were braver than me
Even though they called you *coward*
You, my friend, had escaped
I am still stuck in this space.

You saw heaven first
When we only got a taste
Of eternal life
Can you tell me what it's like?

You were braver than me
I'm left with all these haunting thoughts
That keep me awake at night
Did yours haunt you too?

Life is too short to hurt this way
Believe me, I understand
I'm walking on a wire
That's getting thinner every day.

You were braver than me
Because you balanced on that wire
Until one day it snapped
Down you fell, into an empty cell
And nobody came tumbling in after.

But please know that somebody would have
Had you just given them the chance
Because no matter how alone you felt
You never really were.

There is always somebody
Somebody looking out for you
Somebody waiting for your fall
So, they can be there to help you up
To be there through it all.

You were braver than us
Even though we called you *coward*
You gave up before the help came
But I don't think of you any less.

A Cappella

Because you're braver than me
I cannot pull that trigger
Even if I tried
I cannot say goodbye.

You were able to let go of all the things
All the things that I cannot
The fears that bound you
And heaven found you, just a little too soon.

You're braver than me
But you're okay now
No more pain or tears
I'm stuck in the place you used to be
Broken from the same things.

I made a promise to you a year ago
A promise that I'll keep until the day I die
Because I know today is not my time
And I'll always remember that you were braver than I.

Astronauts

I came to this town not knowing anyone
A young mind and soul prepared to learn
How was I to know that all my stars would soon align?
When I found you in my constellation,
I knew it was a sign.

Like Romeo and Juliet, we were destined to be
Except our story wouldn't end in tragedy
We studied the stars and the galaxies
Even clearer than the telescope, I could see you and me.

If you were an astronaut
We would fly to the moon
Forget about the time passing too soon
I haven't seen your ocean blue eyes for awhile
Frozen in space by the glow in your smile.

The seasons are changing
The leaves turn green again
Spring is here and I'm longing for you
Your quirky jokes, and your spicy attitude
Words cannot begin to express my gratitude.

Like the song by Bruno Mars
Talking to the Moon
I sing it every night trying to get to you
I miss you, my love, why did you have to go?
Did you make it to the moon?
Only you know.

I hope we meet again
I know this isn't the end
Time in space stands still
We will meet again, my friend
How was I to know
That all our stars would align?
From that moment I found you in my
Constellation, I knew it was a sign.

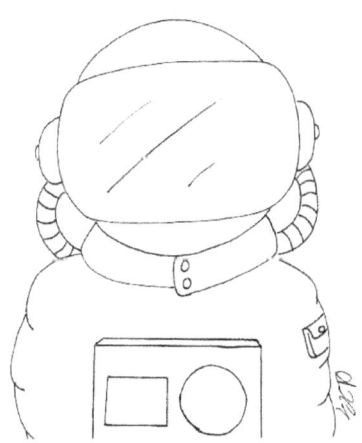

Until We Meet Again

I'm on the inside

And you're on the out

Hope you're thinking of me
I have my doubts.

My in the clouds

Hoping to find you
Inside my dreams
I find sleep.

Fingers to the glass
KNOCK, KNOCK, KNOCK
I pray that it's you
The day never felt so l   o   n   g
I need you.

So close yet we're out of

                                        reach.

I want to feel your hands, I miss you.
Does the clock move
When you tell it to?
Do the minutes move
And listen to you?

Sunrise to sunset
I hope you are my forever
Needing a hand to hold
Always together.

Through the good times
And sad times
Times I don't want to live at all
Times when I'm weak
All I want to do is crawl.

When you're on the inside

I'm on the out

I'll always have you in my mind
No room for doubts

My HEAD in the clouds

We will find a way, until we meet again someday.

I Wrestled a Bear

I wrestled with the bear
It tried to pull my hair
We wrestled to the ground
Nobody heard the sound
Of the roar escape my lungs.

I fought with the lion
No light on in the den
God sewed their mouths shut
They had no chance to win.

I swam with the sharks
They flashed their teeth
I sank to the bottom
Alone in the dark beneath.

The darkness opened its mouth
Swallowed me whole
In the belly of the whale
For three whole days.

Then it spit me out
I landed back on shore
I learned my lesson
And don't fight bears anymore.

Bruises

I am bruised
Blacks and yellows
But I do not let it show.

Bright as the morning sun
Black as his gun
Awakens and burns.

Black as night
Haunting and cautious
Whispers *I do not know.*

I am bruised
Purples and blues
Blooms like spring.

Purple like lilacs
Soap and cologne
I am alone.

Blue like midnight
Laughter and tears
Stained on the pillow.

I am bruised
Secrets and lies
Beneath blue eyes.

Green and orange
Changing like autumn
I am not your girl.

Held your hand
But it's been borrowed
A time, or maybe two.

Running back and forth
Blue, yellow, purple, black
You can't take it back.

I am leaving tonight
Goodbyes and some
Words I can't seem to say.

I can't hide the bruises
They are on display
No more games.

Blues turning black
Forgotten "I love you's"
I wish I could take back.

I am bruised
Blacks, blues, and yellows
But I'll never let them show.

A Cappella

I Am

Very weird
Skinny mini
Older sister
Loves TV
Chatty Cathy
Stylish
Wants sleep
Types fast
Dancing queen
Panda freak
Wears L.E.I. jeans
Plays house
Likes to read
Hates bugs
Root beer
Paints nails
Writes songs
Poetry too
I am.

I Am

Mother, daughter
Sister, wife
Clumsy, talented
Gifted, life
Writer, dreamer
Singer, dancer
Creative, believer
Lover, giver
Forgiver, keeper
Quiet, strong
Right, wrong
Explorer, safe
Home, belongs
Adventurer
Reserved, free
Faith-filled
Woman, person
Girl, warrior
I am.

The Garden

In the garden there is love
A love that brings you close to me
The flowers in the garden, the beauty that I see
The soil in the ground is the light in my soul
Peace is kept here--love is all around.

Speechless

The words don't fit the lines
On this double-sided notebook
They **s m r a e c b l** and hurry
Like busy shuffling feet.

The words can't rhyme
The trial was denied
Even though the words spelled *murder*
Nobody ever heard her.

Broken, black, and blue
Let these words come back to you
The ink will bleed through these sheets
Permanent like a tattoo.

With shuffling feet
And sweaty hands
Like the guilty waiting at the stand
I knew you wouldn't understand.

The words get stuck
In the dark crevices of my mind
They beg to creep out
But I usually leave them behind.

IT CRESCENDOS

If only you knew
The chaos inside my mind
Would you rewind
The passing of time?

The pages write themselves
This is my story **not** yours
What if I told you I've run out of words?
What is there left for me to say?

Tomorrow

If I could hide away
In this space of in between
Pain isn't allowed here
No room for broken tears.

Wade through the tiny cracks
One foot at a time
To cure this heart of mine
From fully breaking.

Truth is at the door
Open it up, there's no going back
I'd give anything, all of me
To see you once more.

Tell you everything
Not waste a single dream
Because all that's left
Are boxes of pictures
That don't mean anything.

All I see is the ghost of you
In every corner, every letter
That we used to write together
I don't know how to go from here.

IT CRESCENDOS

I held you high
High above myself
Now I've taken the fall
I can't tell what's left.

Life is sweet
Until it comes to an end
A chapter closed
The End.

I know I'll see you again
But I'm still healing
From this heartache
I think I'll stay here awhile.

In this space of in between
No room for lost or broken things
No pain or sorrow, just the hope for tomorrow
Because in one of my tomorrow's
I'll be seeing you.

The Sun Will Never Rise

I wish that I could tell you
That you mean everything
But it would be breaking me more
Than the words I write.

I wish that it were simple
To earn someone's trust
But I would be breaking the rules
If I keep insisting that I must.

My thoughts are starting to slow down
So is this weak heart of mine
You remind me to slow down
But not everything is fine.

I cannot see a clear view
I'm tangled up in the vines
I'm saying goodbye this time
The sun will never rise.

If only I could form the right words
I feel them resting on the tip of my tongue
I'm holding my breath, air in my lungs
I just need to let it all go.

IT CRESCENDOS

If only I could see through the glass
I'd say it all straight to your face
But I don't have the courage to say
My heart says stay, but I'm walking away.

I can't see clearly at all
Can't even remember the fall
Love, we gave it our all
But it's goodbye this time
The sun will never rise.

If only it were simple to make the change
Is it my lonely heart that needs replaced?
Locked inside an empty cage
Passion turned into rage.

My thoughts have slowed down
I've lowered my crown
It's time I lived life for *me*
No longer caged, I am free.

I've strengthened the vine
Letting go this time
You can try to drag me down
But down I refuse to go.

Silly boy, didn't you know?
The sun will still rise for me.

Where Did I Go?

Only time can change what words cannot
I speak my mind with every thought
Sinking through what is pulling me in
Reaching out a hand, can you hear me?

Trapped inside a four-walled glass
Shouting to the people that pass
They look my way as if they know
But nobody knows where I go.

I looked up to you because you're all I had
I never knew myself to want something so bad
My feet are in sinking sand dragging me down
Will anyone see me if I try and make it out?

Who am I and where did I go?

Home

I was 8 years old when I learned to ride a bike
Not soon after, I flew my first kite
I remember sunny skies
Meant Mom took us to the park.

Cuddles in the night
When I was afraid of the dark
The crazy beating of my eager heart
Because I was home.

Hearing my favorite song on the radio
The echo of my ballet shoes
To the beat of my cardio
Summer crushes, strawberry lemonade
Left stains on my heart and inside my brain.

But what I loved most of all
Was the reminder that I was home,
Where I belonged.

The meaning of home changed when I was 14
I packed my bags and left everything
Goodbye my friends, goodbye to the memories
I wore my heart upon my sleeve
And writing became my only sense of relief.

A Cappella

I wrote stories I pretended were real
I wrote until it was all I could feel
I lost myself inside the depths of the ink
And slowly I started to sink.

Then one day I was okay again
It started out slow, as life blossomed with a new friend.
I learned I could begin again
And discovered a new meaning to home.

I've lived many places over the years
I've loved, and lost, and fought tears
I've won and lost the war all the same
But I always return to the same place.

I'm older, wiser, and new
I'm a wife, mother, and friend
And no matter how many places I've been
I always find myself at home in the end.

Turn on the Lights, Monsters are Out Tonight

I refuse the medicine
I refuse the pills
This house is suffocating
But I enjoy its thrills
I refuse my bed
And the time of sleep
This house keeps me awake
Alive in my dreams.

I refuse the comfort
Of luxury
I like cold and alone
Feet sticking out over the sheets.

Time dances sensually against the walls
Singing songs of sorrow and casting out fears
I'm listening for the calls
That are found underneath the sheets
It's where the monsters are hiding
Underneath my pillow
That's where they go
That's where they go.

There's a cry out in the middle of the night
I can't tell if it was one of theirs or mine
I toss and turn
And dream and dream

The notes in my head rest upon the bed
I only dream--- I don't sleep.

I dream of you
        (In my sleep)
I dream of you
        (When I'm awake)
I dream of you
        (Every single day)

I can't escape these images that are on replay.

Time stands alone
The movements are slow
I watch the hands on the clock
Slow motion, in the afterglow
Time stands still
I hear it softly
            TICK, TOCK
Shadows on my wall
Slowly creeping down the hall
Watching it move
Under and over and under and over
They are coming soon.

There's a monster hiding out
From underneath my pillow
And inside my window
        KNOCK, KNOCK
My heart is pounding loudly inside my chest
These dreams are keeping me alive
No time to rest
There are monsters in my room
And in my bed and in my head
There are monsters in my head
And I cannot sleep.

Solid Ground

I couldn't see the sunshine
Thorns were caught in the way
I couldn't find happiness
Instead, I hid myself away.

I have been walking with the darkness
Often making the wrong turns
But I must keep on walking
Or I'll crash and burn.

In hope of finding a light
I must learn wrong from right
I can't give in tonight
I may be weak, but I've still got some fight.

From the moment I met with your eyes
I felt something change deep inside
I couldn't close my mind
I could only let you in.

When I was down you reminded me
That there is still more light to be found
My little hope and faith are keeping me sound
I keep searching for solid ground.

When I'm with you, I feel courage
That I didn't know I had
You give me something to look forward to
You give me strength inside my heart.

But when I'm alone
Fear comes rushing back home
Trying to hold on
While slowly letting go
Something is missing
Little did I know, it would be You.

You are there to remind me
Of whom I really am
When I get in the way
You gently whisper to me.

You fill my heart
In a way nobody else can
You're all I'll ever need
Anytime, anywhere.

I discovered myself again
When you revealed what real love is like
You took my heart inside your hands
Made me new and gave me a fresh start.

A Cappella

Everything in me, I found in You
When I am lost, you bring me back to You
I know that with You
I'm forever on solid ground,
A love unimaginable until it's finally found.

White

Awoken from a daydream
The light returns to me
Clean slate---brilliance
Like wings from an angel, I soar
Marshmallow clouds of fluffy white
Rain like crystals and pearls
Cooling like a gentle snow
Frozen---but complete.
There is peace in the freefall
Submerged---full body under
Eyelids shut but I sense a quiet light
Candles glowing---radiance
Unafraid and daring
I am the lion's roar
Echoing off the tiled ceiling
White fan whistling
I am thirteen
Two small doves outside
Hovering just above my window
Innocent and pure
Like the child I was
Wash me clean
So, I can be brand new
Pure, solid, and
White.

A Cappella

You're the One

You're the one
I've been waiting for
You've changed my life
Made me feel like something more.

You've shut out the darkness
And brought forth the light
You've held me close
In the middle of the night.

You've brought me happiness
Like I've never felt before
My heart has changed
I'm walking through a different door.

Here I am, take me into your arms
Waiting for the day
You'll be coming back for me
You're the one I want; I'm not going anywhere.

Tender kisses in my hair
Butterflies nest in my stomach
You took away my despair
When I thought I was beyond repair.

IT CRESCENDOS

Distance doesn't matter when you're in love
No matter how far I can feel you near
Your name is engraved inside my heart
The love that I receive is a work of art.

Here I am, take me into your arms
I'll be waiting for the day, you return to me
You're the one I want, so here I'll wait
I'm not going anywhere.

Nobody else will do
They can't give me the kind of love
That I've given to you
You're the one worth waiting for.

Friend

What would life be without a friend?
What if we always held grudges
And never made amends?
What would life be without a friend?

Time is too short to be on your own
Day by day, every hour the same
With no one to love, you're without a home
We all need someone we can call by name.

Someone to call when you can't sleep at night
A familiar voice, a smile that never fades
Someone who listens when things aren't okay
A shoulder to cry on when you've lost your way.

What would life be without a friend?
Because in a single moment it could all end.

Aurora

She sits quietly along the risen pavement
Crouched down low
Her favorite color is green
The only color she knows
Bored and lonely through the long hours
But happy and pleased when it's time to leave.

Fire burns inside her heart
But there's only one person
That can make her move
Her feet are quick like lightning
As she races along the familiar streets.

She has a place she calls home
But she's rarely there
Born for adventure and wind in her hair
Always on the go, always moving
Steady, but never slow, ready for the show.

Who is this mysterious wonder you may ask?
It's quite simple,
And you might even laugh
She's green and mighty,
and ages like a fine
wine,
Aurora, a beauty,

first car of mine.

The Wreckage

Foot on the pedal
Hands on the wheel
If hazard meant a warning
Then I'd wake up in the morning
And realize the damage we've caused.

Caution lines drawn
But it's too late for that
Foot on the gas
Hands on the wheel
Let's get out of here.

Do I make you nervous?
The way my hands sweat
I pass regrets
And I keep secrets.

Do you believe me?
Will we make it out alive?
I just came along
For the joyride.

What if I can't promise
Something that is concrete?
Looking back in the rearview
Do we go back down that street?

If hazard meant a warning
And time could stand still
Why are we wasting time?
Racing toward our fears.

Foot on the pedal
I can smell the burning metal
We are destined to crash
We were never meant to last.

Pieces of the wreckage
Now a page in the past
Our love, darling
Nothing but a car crash.

Ballad

(bal-lad)

A STORY TOLD BY POEMS OR SONGS

May Fever

I must go back to my home again
To the lovely grass and a bright blue sky
All I ask is to be that child again
A young, bold heart to steer me by.

I feel the rhythm of the swing
Tiny, childlike curls bouncing in the breeze

Innocence

Small shadows flicker across my face
As the sunshine whispers   *Hello*

I must go back to my home again
Where I didn't know a stranger
As we danced in the streets
Wild visions in our heads
Friends with anyone we'd meet.

Wide-eyed and daydreaming
Heart of gold, ready to be

Learning

The melody of the squeaky swings
Close your eyes so you could fly
I could be anybody
Nobody to tell me otherwise.

IT CRESCENDOS

I must go back to my home again
To the colorful happy days
Where skies stayed blue
Wrapped in "I love you's."

I wished it all away too soon
I let it go like a child with a balloon
Like the setting sun at the end of an

Afternoon

The drip-drop of a popsicle on a summer night
Hugs from Mom and tickle fights with Dad
If only I knew then all that I'd had
Before there was good and then the bad.

If I were a child at home
again
I'd wake up, enjoy the
mundane.
Early in the morning
At the beginning of the day,
A day like any other--- in
the middle of May.

Yesterday

In a field like this
Colors bursting all around
As the sun fills the room
I tremble at the sound.

We tried to use our wings
But couldn't lift off the ground
Instead, we sat in wonder
Wondering if tomorrow would come.

We held our breath
Breathing clouds into the glass
I drew pictures of us
Thirty years from now
Trying to imagine what we'd be like.

Eyes so blue
But our jeans a faded gray
That's when it occurred to me
Today is an ordinary day.

We put our shoes back on
And walked all the way to heaven
Like tiny red balloons

You floated away UP, UP, UP, UP
I could not catch you or remind you to stay.
I let you float away.

IT CRESCENDOS

There was a slight tug
On the strings of my heart
But I untied the knots
And somehow it was okay.

I came across my ship
Where I had sailed it last
Climbed aboard
And didn't look back.

I cast the memories
Out in the sea
Watched them sink
Down below me.

down,
down,
down.

Despite feeling far away from you
I tried to keep my heart from turning blue
Yesterday we were searching for today
Today I found myself wishing for more
yesterdays.

94

The Prophylactic Drug

They put a prophylactic drug in my eyes
The day I was born
I cried until I had nothing left
With the prophylactic in my eyes
Sucking out the black
And twisting into the green
They must do it for the thrill
Do they care if I scream?

I feel it slowly crawling down my throat
And clogging up my nose
My head is spinning like a Ferris wheel
People are whirling around
I feel something tingly inside my veins
Am I waking up?
Or is this all a dream?
Do they notice me here?
Tiny and helpless.

They put a prophylactic drug in my eyes
They said it was good for me
But was it all a lie?
It should be wearing off soon
But do they really know?
I want to leave this place
Where is my mom?

IT CRESCENDOS

My head feels fuzzy
And my eyes are blurry
Is it a side effect or am I still crying?
Mom where are you?

I cry because that's my only way of reaching
But my own cry stings my ears
I scream until I know someone is near
But why isn't it *you*? Who are *they*?
Where are you when I need you?
Mommy, I'm not okay.

Finally, they tell me someone named Mommy
And Daddy have come to see me
But I can't keep my eyes open any longer
I'm getting sleepy
I miss you, please hold me
I'll see you soon when I'm awake.
I just hope this part wasn't a mistake.

I close my eyes and rest them in my head
They whisper words to me I can't comprehend
Maybe if I could teach them my language
Then they would understand
And maybe someday I can learn theirs too
But this is enough for one day
If only I had the final say.

The Great Gatsby

There's a great tale about a man of heart
But tragically so, his life fell apart
With a smile so contagious and eyes of gold
The love for another, his poor heart couldn't hold.

He lived in a place by the name of West Egg
In love with the girl,
He would soon have to beg
To fall back in love with him
Because chances were slim.

When a man without riches
Moved in next door
A life of surprises could only
Lead to something more.

They quickly became friends
And Nick brought him Daisy
Daisy admired Gatsby,
While Nick saw him as crazy.

Gatsby took his chances
Had to face his fears
They moved too fast, then came the tears
Tom, Daisy's husband, was furious at the sight
Though Tom was a cheater,
Something didn't feel right.

Then, one night, one of Tom's good friends'
Wife had been killed by Gatsby
And he wanted revenge
Wilson found Gatsby relaxing by his pool
With a single shot, he killed the fool.

So ends this tragic tale
Of a man and his expenses
Who had little friends,
But plenty of riches.

Though his life was short
And love didn't last
Time and memories
Take us back to the past.

Next time you think of
Driving through West Egg
Remember what happened
But don't let it go to your head.

Think of Great Gatsby
And the things he has done
And the man he could have been
If pride hadn't won.

The Waiting Post

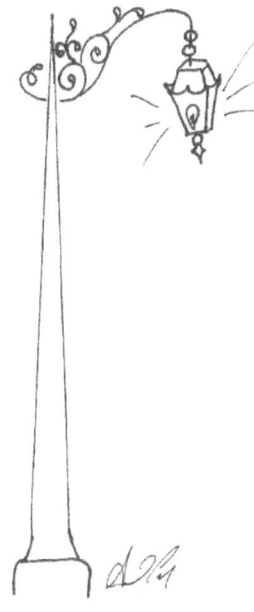

Calm like the sea
Inside I'm a raging storm
Lighthouse glows
Come find me.

Message in a bottle
But you're hard to read
Encrypted notes
That I'm trying to see.

Bright like a kaleidoscope
All the colors
Twists and turns
I want to learn.

Burning like a fire
A flame that never dies
My desire
The flames are rising higher.

Fire and ice
You burn while I shiver
Silver and gold
Flowing like a river.
The bird and his song
We hum along
Trees sway

IT CRESCENDOS

And I whisper, "Please stay."

More colors and the sun sets
Time to go, time for rest
I'll be here waiting when tomorrow comes
With the wake of the morning sun.

Our feet are quick
Telling us to run
But our hearts tell us to stay
Here at the waiting post.

Raindrops

It was a long day and I needed rest
I made dinner and laid in bed
I lay there wondering when you'll be home
I left the porch light on.

When I tried to close my eyes
My whole life flashed before me
It made me stop and think
Where am I really going?

I closed my eyes
And folded my hands
Got down on my knees and prayed
That's when it started to rain.

I said, "Lord thank you for this day,
And all that you have made
Thank you for my beautiful daughter
And the memories that'll never fade."

"Thank you for my dear husband,
Please help him to get home safe
I know that I'm not perfect
But I'm doing the best that I can...
Thank you for the rain, Amen.

IT CRESCENDOS

Then the house was dark and quiet
Quiet except the whisper of the rain
Dancing along the windows
And in the shadows of my faith
Washing away the pain from yesterday.

It had been a while
Since I had talked to God
Sometimes I keep Him close
And other times He's tucked away.

But tonight, I need Him closer than ever
So close I can feel
His breath upon my shoulder
And I find myself on my knees again.

I have been through many trials
And I know that there will be more
Lord, sometimes I just want to turn away
It's so much easier to walk right out the door.

You know exactly where my heart is
Lord, you know my every thought
You handcrafted all these raindrops
And will guide me to the path that I should go.

Ballad

That's when I heard my husband's truck
Pulling into our drive, I ran outside
I gathered him into my arms
And together we cried.

"Lord, thank you for this day,
And all that you have made
Thank you for our children
And the memories that'll never fade."

"Thank you for our marriage,
Thank you, God, for forgiving us
In blood of your perfect Son
Washing away all the things we've done."

With our heads to the sky
Hands and hearts wide open
Let the Heavens pour down
Heavenly rain.

And I can't help but say,
Thank you, Lord, for the rain.

The Canvas

Close your eyes
What does your canvas paint for you?
Do the colors bleed into one another?
Or can you see straight through?

Golds, red, purples, and blues
All my life I've painted pictures
Separate pieces of one big image
Trying to figure out how they all fit together.

Close your eyes
Don't move or think, just breathe
What do you see?
Tell me because I want to know.

Turn me upside down
Shake me around
Take me somewhere new and exciting
I want to be lost and then found.

Inside this midnight hour
Dark like a Milky Way
Mind racing, heart skipping
Paint me a picture.

A Catch in the Wind

You are so beautiful
But you will never be mine
So incredible
But we are tangled up in the vine.

So unforgettable
But I have to this time
So unreachable
Little angel of mine.

I try to run
But you keep pulling me

under.

Under your skin
I try to love you
But you will not let me in
My words are nothing more
Than a catch in the wind.

You are so complicated
You have chains on your heart
So frustrating
And it's tearing me apart.

IT CRESCENDOS

Everything feels twisted
Like a roaring tornado
Everything out of order
And then you call out my name.

Forward, backwards
Running, running
Upside down, no direction
Running out of time.

I try to run
But you are one step ahead
Pulling me under
You get under my skin.

I try to love you
But with you I cannot win
My words mean nothing
Nothing more than a catch in the wind.

Without You (Alone)

When I look back at you
I'm looking back to what we had
Staring inside a glass
That I never could see through
Now it's all making sense

d
  o
    w
      n

                          I go, and everybody knows it.

I'm falling apart
I can't rewind
Everything that I was
Now it's all behind me.

I can't start over
I can't go under
I can't go around it
I've got to go through it.

I'm hurting inside
I can't sleep at night
Thinking about what's been said
Too much movement inside my head.

d
  o
   w
    n

                       I go, and everybody knows it.

Two separate worlds
We're divided in two
What we once were | Now alone without you.

Where do I go from here?
Where is there left to go?
Two separate thoughts
There's me | And there's you.

Two separate minds
One of a kind
Now we can't see
What we're running into.
Me, alone without you.

What did I do
To wish you away?
What did I say
To make you feel this way?

Ballad

Why isn't sorry
Ever enough?
Why can't we hurry
And make things up?

Thinking about what's been said
Too much movement inside my head
All this empty space
And a cold empty bed.

The Orange Tree (*In Memory of Will)*

It started out as a tiny seed
Which later grew into a tree
I watched it grow and grow and grow
Until it grew ten times taller than me.

Colors of orange
Started to burst from the leaves
My mouth began to water
And I grinded my teeth.

Each day I'd go outside
To check on the tree
Waiting patiently for the oranges
To grow and grow and grow.

Until one day, the oranges began to fall
I did a silly dance and clapped my hands
I grabbed the ladder
I had resting against the house
And began to climb and climb and climb.

I climbed up I made it to the top
The highest point in the tree
And oh, how beautiful and ripe they were!
They seemed as if they glistened
And sang to me!

I reached out to touch one
But I saw to my surprise
The orange looked at me
As it came to life!

It growled at me in anger
And almost bit my nose!
I tried to keep my balance
But I was wobbling on my toes.

The tree started to sway madly
And it hung me from my drawers
It hissed and snarled and laughed at me
And suddenly, I wasn't hungry anymore.

A Stranger's Secret

Threatened by the shadows
I find myself running once again
Running from the demons
That have taken over my dreams.

When I'm awake, beads of sweat
Pour down my face like a quiet rain
Letting my eyes slowly come into focus
I can't escape the cries from my own pain.

My mother comes rushing in
Her face, flushed--- eyes, hallowed in
I can't hear what she's saying
But I sense her worry
I close my eyes and wish myself away.

But away is where she'll send me
If I don't pull my act together
Like she's told me many times before
But I'm scared to go away forever.

If lonely were a color
I'd be every shade of gray
And with the wind
I'd crumple like dust and blow away.

Ballad

My friends think I'm acting
Merely putting on a mask and playing the part
But who ever said that living was easy?
Nobody ever warned us
That it would be so hard.

When you have felt the way that I have
All you can imagine is an escape
But not the kind others imagine for me
I cannot live my life inside their prison.

I am human just like you
I have wings and I want to fly
Just please try and understand
Why it would be so much easier
To give up and end this life.

I made a promise
Not only to you but myself
And if I promise I'll get better
Do you promise not to get me help?

I'm looking out my window
And today the sun is shining
There is hope in today
As I watch the tiny bluebird fly away.

And I think to myself
Someday, I'll fly away too
Someday, I'll learn how to fly
Hopefully, someday soon.

The Grand Opening
(Inspired by the Netflix Documentary Bad Vegan*)*

I can't tell you what I'm thinking
Because I don't know
It won't make any sense
Don't ask and I won't tell.

All I know is who I once was
A young girl with big dreams
Bright, but a little naive
But I made her leave.

Now I'm picking up pieces
From the mess you made
The mess we made, I made
I said sorry but it'll never be enough.

I was never enough for you
All the crazy you made me do
I did for me, did for you
Thought you really loved me too.

I fell hard and I fell fast
I set you so high, too high
We were destined to crash
And we burned, I burned
The tables got turned.

Lesson learned
But who can I trust?
I was somebody
Now nothing but dust.

I'm not stupid
But I did some stupid things
He was a diamond
He was my shiny thing.

But you wouldn't understand
Thought it was all planned
But I did not rehearse this part
I watched my life crumble like sand.

At the hands of another
He built my walls
And then knocked them down
I came tumbling down, we tumbled down.

I never meant to hurt anyone
But in return I hurt everyone
He hurt me, and I hurt them
Like dominoes one after another.

I have a story to tell
If you'll take the time to listen
I'd tell the me then, what I know now
If it could change everything somehow.

Ballad

I'd turn back time
And I'd never give him a dime
Protect this little heart of mine
That I don't know how to mend.

I'd keep those to me close
And my friends always near
I'd give them my all
If they were still here.

If you're out there
If you're still listening
I do think about you
And hope someday, maybe
Just maybe... we could start again.

Unseen

My hand trembles
As it rests gently on your door
A place I know so well,
I wish when I walked in time froze still.

The room dark and cold
Once full of warm memories
I could once hold
Along with you in my arms.

My heart is torn
My faith is shaken
Will I ever feel whole again?
The way you made me feel.

I believed in miracles
I trusted in the impossible
I got down on my knees
For as long as I was able.

I pled with a God
I see and know is faithful
I know He heard my cries
As I wept at the mourning table.

Ballad

Surrounded by others
Who had cheered and praised with me
Day and night we would lift our hands
To a Savior we knew had the power to save.

But what do you do when He doesn't?
How do you accept the path He has chosen?
It isn't fair, God---Why, God?
This wasn't a part of *my plan.*

You gave me the faith to pray
You gave me the faith to remain
You gave me hope
That someday I'd kiss my baby's face again.

But I'm forgetting your greatest miracle
I'm afraid that might be my biggest mistake.

You sacrificed the ultimate price
The cost for our sins,
Through the life of your Son
He paid a death that wasn't deserved or fair
And yet He conquered death for all of us.

You were brought back to life, Jesus
Your Father raised You from the dead!
And even though, the miracle that I prayed
Wasn't the miracle you had in mind.

IT CRESCENDOS

My heart breaks with my own loss
But in the wreckage, I can still see hope
Hope in the same Father that loves and saves
Because He defeated His own grave!

Hope that my child is with Jesus in Heaven
Happy and free from all pain
In a place where no harm can reach her
A place someday I too, long to be.

With my hand on the door
I know what I'll find the moment I walk inside
And while there is pain in today,
I have hope and joy in tomorrow.

My Jesus didn't forsake me
My Jesus didn't abandon me
My Jesus will be with me for all my days
Until we meet face to face.

I believe I will see my sweet daughter
United and free we shall be
My human heart my never understand,
All the things of the unseen.

Ballad

Keep my spirit alive
For as long as you'll have me here
Wipe my tears and help me to find
Glimpses of joy in the middle of *here.*

Continue to ignite my flame
For in the dark shines a light
Because pain isn't eternal for those
Who have set their heart right.

Keep me grounded
Even though my feet may shake
Until the last breath that I take
Remind me of the miracle and hope
Of your coming day.

Until then, I'll continue to pray
I will pray, pray, pray, pray.

Running in Place

Where can we run?
When we've got no place to go?
Where can we hide?
When we just want to be alone.

Lost and confused
Running in place
Don't know which way is UP
My brain is in space.

It's been a long day
I can't think anymore
Tired of the people
Tired of feeling ignored.

How did I become so out of place?
Out of touch
Am I losing the race?

Surrounded by fear
Loneliness is near
Why won't you pick up the phone?
Have you gone away too?

Ballad

Then I hear you calling
You're calling out my name
I turn around but find nothing
Everything appears the same.

Yet somehow, I can *feel* it
I feel your warm embrace
It's like you're holding me tight
And you don't let me go.

Too tired to argue
Too tired to fight
Sick of losing
Sleep at night.

You whisper you love me
That you'll love me forever
You're here to save me
Here to bring me back home.

I was lost and confused
I was running in place
Didn't know which way was UP
My brain was in space.

IT CRESCENDOS

All I knew was this wasn't the end
I let you carry me in your arms
Like I would a close friend
I may not be ready yet to face my mistakes
But someday, someday soon.

In Loving Memory *(For Uncle Tim)*

I know it's hard to let you go
With every day that goes by
And it's hard to understand
The reason that you died.

With pictures only as memories
It's so hard without you here
But I know I'm not alone
I have nothing I should fear.

The days will carry on
As will the years
My boys will be growing old
And looking more like you.

One day they'll be proud to call themselves
DAD
And they'll tell their kids
About the great one they had.

There won't be a day I don't shed a tear
Because I'll forever remember all the years
All the good and bad together we've gone through---
There's not a moment in my life
That I won't dedicate to you.

I've loved you for all my life
Please know that I still do
With every passing day
I'm seeing more and more of you.

One day I'll too see Heaven
All my pain will fade away
No tears to cry, my eyes will dry
And together we'll be again.

One day we'll be in Heaven
Looking back at where we were
I'll fill you in with all these years
That you missed while you weren't here.

I'll love you forever
Because you're my forever,
And forever you'll be in our hearts.

Ballad

Places I've Been

You don't know the places I've been
The nights I've spent on my own
Praying for it all to end.

You gave me shelter and let me in
Accepted me for all that I am
But you haven't been where I have been.

I wish that I knew how to open up
Like the blossoming of a flower
But it's going to take some time.

There's only one person that I trust
We've been through it all together
We were dealt a bad hand, but that's life.

You don't know the places I've been
Or the past that I'm running from
There are pieces of me that you'll never see
Because there are places, I can no longer go.

This is me trying to spread my wings
I've been given a fresh start
I wanted to thank you, sincerely
From the bottom of my broken heart.

I've learned so much
But I am still learning
My dreams can be reached
If I keep yearning.

You haven't been where I have been
But to me, you've been my greatest friend
And because of your kindness,
Please know that this won't be my ending.

Goodbyes are Harder than I Thought

I wish I could tell you how I really feel
All the pain and hurt inside is real
I wish that I could see us the way it was before
When we were in love, and I loved you more
I am breaking, I am changing,
I am not the same.

I wish that I could say that I still love you
But those three little words feel far away
We'd say them to each other every day,
But now it is not the same
I cannot say them to your face.

I wish that I could tell you
Where things went wrong
I held your heart in the palm of my hands
For far too long
Now I am balancing on a tightrope
And I can no longer hold on.

I wish that I could be the one to catch you
The one that was always supposed to love you
But lately, I've been thinking too much
About what my heart wants and what is pure.

IT CRESCENDOS

I wish that I still felt the same around you
The way we would hold hands
And my heart would skip a beat
But now I am split at the seams
Chasing other dreams.

I wish that I weren't the one to break your heart
The biggest part of you now torn apart
Tossed into a sea with your emotions
And I cannot stand to watch you sink.

I wish that I were able to start this over
If only I knew a way to make this right
Would you even take my hand,
If I held it out to you like a lifeline?
Would it feel just like the old times?

I wish that I had all the answers
Because if I did, I'd give them all to you
All I know is that we need to go
Our separate ways
But I won't leave with a whole heart.

There are many things I wish I could say
I can't turn back time to a different day
No words could mend the hurt, or make it all okay
But I hope someday you are.
I still wish a lot of things for you
But most of all, I wish you the best.

The Island

I love the pieces
That don't fit together

When I fix my hair
It does not fair
With the weather.

My clothes hardly match
I never carry cash
But I'm not broke
I've got a hidden stash.

I talk quietly
And listen to words
I'd rather not speak
Then pretend I'm being heard.

I take notes
I notice the small things
I don't forget
I'm not amused with shiny rings.

I keep to myself
But I want to let you in
It's hard to sometimes
When I feel myself giving in.

IT CRESCENDOS

I don't ask for much
I don't expect in return
I am polite when I ask
And I always wait my turn.

I am human
Somedays it really shows
But there's a part of me
That only fear knows.

I am a fragment
Of a greater whole
I can't see through the window
There's a fog inside my brain.

I am the pieces
That do not fit together
I am the eye of the storm
Upsetting the weather.

I need someone to calm my sea
Come and rescue me
This will be my last message in a bottle
I hope it reaches somebody.

I have been here all this time
Alone on the island
I'll be here lost at sea
Somebody please rescue me.

The Anchor

Standing on the edge
Waiting to let go
Deciding what is real
Do I dare dive in below?

The waters are calm
I am a raging sea
I close my eyes
So, I can breathe.

You are the ship
I am the anchor
Pulling us down
          down.

We fell into the deep
Far below
From where we used to be
And where we should be.

I try to speak
But it comes out an echo
It bounces off the waves
And then sinks into the deep.

IT CRESCENDOS

You are the ball
I am the chain
Slowly swinging us down
                   down.

I fell too fast and a little too deep
I pulled you in
Now we're starting to sink
A game of tug-o-war that I couldn't win
I pulled too hard, and you fell in.

Standing on the edge
Wanting to let go
Pull me back
Hand me the rope.

The waters are calm
Yet I am a raging sea
Will you be the one to rescue me?

You were the ship
I was the anchor
Trying to pull us down
                   down.

I thought it was over
I was ready to drown
Another soul lost at sea
Never to be found...
But alas, you didn't let me
drown.

Instead, you pulled me
UP
UP
UP.

Going Home

Driving too fast with my windows down
It's starting to rain as I reach the edge of town
I don't have a map, but my bags are packed
I'm heading south, not sure when I'll be back.

I sing the words to my favorite song
When I forget the words, I just hum along
Driving for a while now
Not sure where I am or where I've been
All I know is I'm going home.

I find a place to rest for the night
I say a prayer and close my eyes
I don't wake up until the kiss of the sun
Touches my lips like a cup of coffee
I drink it all in and I'm ready again.

Back on the intersection I'm ready to go
So many places but none were home
I take it all in, enjoy the ride
The journey has just begun.

When I've finally discovered who I am
I can love everything
That's ever blessed these hands
And only God knows my plans.

Ballad

The lines in the road
Remind me of myself
A winding path
I have yet to discover.

Someday I'll have a husband
With a house and kids
When I wake in the morning
I'll be greeted with a kiss.

I won't look back
Wondering what did I miss?
I'll scrap my wishes
And start living it out.

When my kids grow old
And they, too, decide to leave
And find themselves on an open road
I hope something along the way
Brings them on the path back home.

When they look me in the eyes
I'll do my best not to cry
Even though I understand
Because I once was in their shoes.

They'll call me on the phone
And say to me, *Mom I'm going home.*

Roxy

If she didn't make it to Heaven
Then where did she go?
Why did she come into my life,
And then so quickly she had to go?
Do I not deserve to know?
I think I have the right
As a child, a pet was nothing but a dream
Then I turned 14 and my wish came true
But if only I had known, I didn't have a clue
That my silly little dream wouldn't even
Last a year.

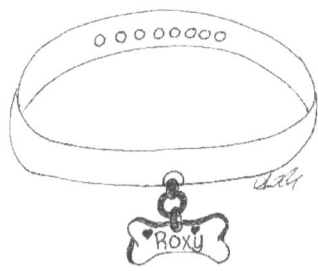

Melody

(mel-uh-dee)

NOTES ARRANGED IN SINGLE NOTE SEQUENCES

Forbidden Love

What if I were to break the mold,
That holds me together?
Let you inside, exposed, without cover
All my pieces, the broken and together
Rain, wind, and shine, any kind of weather.

What if I told you my secrets?
Let you have the key, unlocked, chain-free
All my pieces, the broken and together
Do you still like the me you see?

What if I were to hold your hand?
Would you let me?
Let you feel my warmth, unguarded
Love me for me, waters uncharted.

Would you let me hold you in my arms?
I'd let you embrace me, now and forever
All my pieces, broken and together
You put me together, together again.

But what if we can't break the mold?
What if you are never mine to hold?
What if our love turns to stone?
What if we are better off alone?

One of Those Girls

I want to be one of those girls
A perfect smile and delicate curls
Thin around the waist
Curves that fall in the right place.

I want to be one of those girls
Walks in confidence
Afraid of nothing
Doesn't falter in the spotlight.

She says the right things
Perfect when she sings
Doesn't make mistakes
No room for breaks.

Her path is smooth
She doesn't miss a beat
She always wins
Has never known defeat.

I want to be one of those girls
Only then I would rule the world
If only I could be that perfect girl
But too bad she doesn't exist.

The Angst of Breaking Up

I didn't feel it when you drove away
Didn't feel it the next day
I didn't try to make you stay
I watched us burn up like ashes in a tray.

I didn't feel it when I woke up
Didn't feel it putting on my makeup
I used to feel so much when around you
But now I don't feel anything at all.

Pulling up into my driveway
Our song is on repeat, but it doesn't hit me
I've heard the words a thousand times
And this probably won't be the last.

I walk past the couch we used to lay on
The only place you ever wanted to crash
I can almost see your empty self
Sitting there like you didn't give a damn.

I took all the pictures off the walls
The holes left behind, and all the missed calls
Your favorite shirt, crumpled on the ground
Forgotten like a lost baseball card never found.

IT CRESCENDOS

There's a coffee mug in my kitchen
That I can never drink from again
It was a gift for your birthday
Yet somehow it never got used.

It's been almost three weeks
At night I still toss and turn
I had prayed for you; hoped you were The One
But now I'm left with pictures to burn.

I realize now I wasn't playing fair
Whenever someone would ask *(and they would)*
I'd mostly tell them it was mutual *(which is true)*
But sometimes I'd lie to make myself feel better
And put the blame all on **you.**

But it wasn't fair of you to "ghost" me
Then greet me kindly after the silence
You smiled as though, nothing was wrong
And greeted me with a familiar,
HELLO, GREEN EYES.

A steel knife
Straight through the heart
In the angst of breaking up.

That's when the conversation choked
Because I started to feel too much
But you never felt *enough*
I was a little too much.

I get it, *(really, I do)*
That's just the way it goes sometimes
I'll do better, be smarter, know better
There will always be another *you,*
(But there will <u>never</u> be another **ME**).

The Key

I've got the key in hand
Fingers closed around it
No tears in my eyes
Some things are still in my control.

I can say goodbye
Erase your name
Never write to you again
Because I am coming undone.

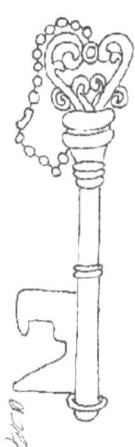

The silliest things
Are gnawing at my brain
I sound a little bit insane
How can I explain?

I can try to forget
But that's the thing
The things that I cannot forget
Are undoubtedly my biggest regrets.

I know, I know, I know
I should let it all go
Slip through the cracks
Out the window.

Melody

No more looking back
I play with Queens
You are just a Jack
Tumbling down, down.

I am looking into a mirror
Trying to see myself clearer
If I could see past the lies
You made me believe.

I've got the key in hand
You don't have to understand
You don't get to be my man
We won't be happily ever after, The End.

I'm like a whisper in the wind
Catch me if you can
I'm just close enough
To be out of your reach.

Still Inspired

Like a vulture stalking its prey
I was picked a p a r t
Piece by piece
        Line
        By
        Line.

A **golden** treasure
I once held dear
No longer mine
But theirs too.

Words I had written
Now in their hands
Suddenly, I was the puzzle
With the m_ss_ng parts.

TheyADDEDwords in
And took   out
     (words)
Words I thought made sense
Suddenly all order of out.

In my mind I was trying to piece
Everythingtogether
But I found myself
Looking at a JMULEBD mess.

When the pages returned
Back into my hands
I wanted to cRuMpLe them UP
And leave the room.

*   *   *

I could feel the HOT stinging tears

                                                    G
                                        N
                            I
                  S
        I
R
From underneath my lids.

But I remained *calm*
I kept my cool
And in that moment
Another cR@Zy, s!LLY, idea struck me!

So, I wrote this poem.

Green-Eyed Girl

Helpless child
Lost inside
Self-pity
And self-doubt.

When she's alone
Tears don't refuse to fall
At times she feels
Like nobody cares at all.

Deep inside the sea
Of the green behind her eyes
A girl that's torn
Ragged and worn.

Sometimes she can't breathe
Tossing, and turning---can't sleep
She tries to move the world
But it's too much for her shoulders.

Speakers blaring, the world is too loud
Favorite pair of blue jeans wearing down
Everything always gets around
When you're from a small town.

Melody

She hears the rumors
They whisper down the hall
Like a ghost she would disappear
The lies made her feel so small.

The pain is real, and so is the hurt
She's become numb, can't seem to heal
The scars on her wrist
Reveal wounds in her heart.

She has a story to tell,
But where would she start?
Time is running out
Like sand pouring in an hourglass.

Sing her one more song
Make her feel like she belongs
Catch her if she falls
Because you know we all do.

She can't carry the weight of the world
She's forgotten who she is
Remind her of the good days,
Take her back in time.

She's fragile, yet beautiful
That, I have no doubt
She's broken, but she's worthy
The green-eyed girl
I used to know.

I Can Play with Fire Too

Mama always told me
Never play with fire
Be careful, you might get burned
But I watched the flames grow higher
She thought that I would never learn.

I came stepping out of the fire
A lesson I should've learned
The tables have turned
Left with another picture to burn.

I held my heart in my hands
I gave it so freely
Thought you would be careful
I labeled it *fragile.*

But somehow it slipped
Right between your fingers
Slippery like the lies
That slid off your tongue.

You were the joker
I was the ace of spades
You laid down your smooth play
But who was I? Worthy of *you?*

You spit me out
Before I could breathe you in
My heart too deep
A promise you couldn't keep.

I couldn't breathe
I couldn't speak
Tongue-tied
Is this defeat?

Man, you had me good
I was the fool
You reeled me in
And I forgot how to swim.

But not anymore
I've locked the doors
If you come knocking
I won't come running.

My mama always told me
Never to play with fire
But I can play this game too
And really, I wish you well.

Next time you cast your spell
It won't be on me
Because the joke's on you
You can go now
And wipe your feet before you leave.

The Highs and Lows

Bitter
Darkness
Falling
Quiet
Nothing.

Kind
Loving
Charming
Kisses
Sweet.

Strange
Unfamiliar
Lost
Confused
Shatter.

Soulmates
Together
Forever
Eternity
Heaven.

Noises
Voices
Louder
Chaos
Scream.

Center
Surrender
Being
Soul
Whole.

Calm
Water
Blue
Vivid
Dream.

Selfish
Green
Greedy
Lustful
Cheating.

Lies	Song
Despair	Sing
Gloom	Shout
Fear	Clap
Darkness.	Joy.
Dark	Fade
Light	Slowly
Day	Quickly
Night	Temporarily
Tomorrow.	Life.

Redemption
Forgiveness
Faith
Joy
Content.

Alive
Well
Thrive
Thankful
Amen.

Tiptoe

If I had known what an angel was
Maybe I wouldn't have made such a mess
The pencil on my desk
Parallel to your finger
You draw blurry lines with.

Wrap me in a song
I want to forget this
Color by number
You're difficult to read
The poison I thought I'd need.

If only I spoke your language
It's a strange dialect
Your voice, barely a whisper
Nothing like I ever heard
You say so much without a word.

Sometimes I get so angry
Fists clenched tight, barred teeth
I can't make you understand
What it's doing to me
You don't see what I see.

Melody

One day you're my sugar sweet
Then you're a cavity in my teeth
I can't spit you out
And let you trickle down the drain.

Walking on eggshells
With my bare feet
I want you, but you're out of reach
I've gotten pretty good at walking on tiptoe.

Arms out for balance
Will you catch me if I fall?
Down, down, like Humpty Dumpty
Who will put me back together, after all?

Remembrances of Me

One day
I'll look back on the scars from my past and say that
I've overcome
One day
I'll have the confidence in me that others place within
me
One day
I'll be standing on the outside looking in and I'll see
beauty within
One day
I'll replace the hate for love, and despair for hope in
things above
One day
I'll be on top of the world, looking down below
And I'll see her, the old me
The skin that I shed
Hello new me
Goodbye old self
One day.

Rescue Me

You were my first, hand to hold
The warmth they left turned to gold
Your eyes deep like the ocean
You came to rescue me.

We danced underneath the stars
We stayed out late counting cars
Your fingers tickled in my hair
Carried the world without a care.

Every day I see a piece of you
Pieces that I'm starting to miss
Tiny fireflies flickering in the night
Blinking into the moonlight.

You were the one that I loved
Now my heart has turned to stone
My world is cold, and I feel alone
Memories erased from my phone.

When we danced underneath the moon
We stayed out late
And slept 'til noon
Everything that was, ended too soon.

IT CRESCENDOS

I would dance with you one last time
Give me one more night
To make me feel alright
I have known you all my life.

Memories will fade
And so will we
I wished you had stayed
But instead, we both gave up.

Falling for You

How do you know when something is real?
When to hold on and when to let go?
I am the anchor on a sail
And I don't want to sink this time.

How close are you before you go too far?
It feels like I am falling
Trying to hold on to something
The things that I know.

It's hard sometimes
When the map isn't clear
Confusion is all around
Yet, I keep you here.

I feel as though I've known you
For what seems like a lifetime
There is something about you
That I cannot turn away from.

I don't know what will happen
Will you stay, or will you go?
I want to be with you
I am not better off on my own.

IT CRESCENDOS

I don't have all the answers
But I do have one thing
I think I'm falling for you
Can you say the same?

The Mountaintop

You find me in the rush
You find me in the fall
You're with me through the highs
You're with me through it all.

You're there in the quiet
In the crevices of my mind
You're there in the present
You're there all the time.

You hear my thoughts unspoken
I don't have to say a word
You are my Creator
Life Giver, and Sustainer.

You catch me when I stumble
And sometimes you don't
I cling to you in my trials
Your love carries me through.

You are the reason that I rise
I'm the reason that I fail
You're with me in the darkest night
Your love always prevails.

IT CRESCENDOS

You stretched your arms open wide
With Your great love for me
Forgiving sins, I hadn't yet committed
By hanging on the tree.

I feel so small when I see it all
Your Word of Life before me
Help me see, the person you see
Worthy, because you declared me to be.

You hold me when I feel weak
You remind me of my strength
Strength that only comes from You
You are my solid rock.

Remind me to see, that this too shall pass
The pain of yesterday, soon to fade away
Guide me through the valley
So, I can see you on the mountaintop.

Cinnamon

It was the way you said my name aloud
The way you made me feel like I was floating
Above the clouds, are we dreaming now?

It was the way you looked at me and grinned
Your laugh, was sweet like cinnamon
The taste still in my lungs, I can breathe you in.

It was the way you held my hand in yours
Comparing size *(we both know it was a joke)*
Nothing but a puppet, I was just for show.

I know better now, than I did when
A little naïve, a little too easy to bend
I wished I'd known now, what I didn't then.

Lips pressed against my cheek
Lips that lied anytime they'd speak
Rehearse your lines, ready to cheat.

Another drink down, I watch as I go
Into the car, down the streets I used to know
Into the black of night, I should have said no.

My head was in a game of tug 'o war
You know the reasons why
You told me it was do or die.

IT CRESCENDOS

We laughed until our bodies begged for sleep
In your arms, but not yours to keep
But I feel alone when I go home.

I always left my light on
Just in case you'd call
Too quick to take the fall.

I don't understand this pull I have
It's like I'm standing in sinking sand
I want to let go, while still holding your hand.

It was the way it felt with your arms around
The warmth and smell of your cologne
Quiet hums from our lungs in the dark.

Sometimes I wished
We could have worked it out
In a perfect world, without any doubts.

Just love, and the sweetest cinnamon.

The Promise

They say that people come, and they go
It's a quick hello, then they're out the door
But you stayed where you stood
And loved me like you said you would.

You give me butterflies
Every time you meet my eyes
I can see that you feel it too
When it's just me with you.

They say I'm moving way too fast
Always digging up the past
I'm praying that this will last
Are you still in it?

There's no one quite like you
The way you make me glow
You send me shivers from head to toe.

I've been through my share of storms
I'm still fighting this tide
You help me be bold and brave
Throughout this wild ride.

IT CRESCENDOS

They say that people come and go
And don't I know *(that may be true)*
But know I love you
That, I can promise you.

Rose

Tears fold in behind her smile
Holding on for a little while
Flaws creased into the depth of her beauty
The mirror only shows her what she wants to see.

Trying to make it through another day
Empty lines of meaningless words
When she goes home, she will find her eyes
And make sure she keeps them dry.

Nobody knows the rivers she cries
She doesn't feel alive,
But doesn't want to die
A broken vase on the inside.

She's as fragile as a branch
She never bends, only breaks
Her lips are as red as the rose
But her heart as dark as it's thorns.

Toxic

You're a poison
Luring me in
Caught in a trap
Tangled within.

The taste of your lips
Stings against my skin
Arms around me
The sweetest sin.

I shouldn't want you
You know you're not my type
My heart screams yes!
While my head shouts *danger, danger!*

Laying there laughing
Are we innocent?
Naïve and young
I don't know what I don't know.

Part of me wants you
Wants you so bad
But love, we both know
You're a love that will never last.

It won't be long
Until you pack your bags
That's how you are
Always ready to leave.

I should let you go *(this time)*
You're toxic for me, I know
My heart knows better now
Yet, I just can't say no.

The part of me that wants you
Wants you so bad
Wants a taste of all the things
I've never had.

You're like a poison
Luring me in
Drink you up
Refill my cup.

The taste of your lips
Stings against my skin
I want to let you in
But I shouldn't give in.

I can't say no
When I'm lying in your bed
Our eyes closed
Your hand behind my head.

IT CRESCENDOS

You're a leech
You won't let go
Time is wasting
I should really go.

I can't stay here *(not anymore)*
I can't stay the night
I wish I hadn't caved
This doesn't feel right.

I really should go
I won't be back
Stop luring me in
Getting me off track.

I wish I believed my own words
You're toxic and my heart knows
You're no good for me
Yet, I can't say no.

High School Drama Queen

Wide awake, you keep me up in bed
I've got one hundred different things
Running through my head
It's hard to fall asleep,
When all your dreams are dead.

Let's run away to a place
Where the air tastes like rain
And the sun shines like Sunday morning
You bring your laugh,
And I'll bring my dry sense of humor.

We can taste the days
One at a time
I like simple songs with pretty words
I tried my hand at poetry
But forgot the words to rhyme.

Hello, stranger
Do you remember how we met?
Do you think of me?
Or am I just a memory
That you tend to forget?

I don't know how to do this
I don't know how to make us work
Let's just be friends
Let's pretend we're all OK.

I stopped throwing coins into the fountain
Making wishes that didn't come true
Roses may be red, and I may still love you
But you don't have a clue
That's just what you do.

High school changes people
Some for the better
Some for the worse
It's too soon to grow up
I thought I knew you better than I do.

We don't realize what we have until it's gone
It's hard to say *I'm sorry* and then move on
We often hurt the ones closest to our hearts
And the most foolish things tear us apart.

I don't mean to be a high school drama queen
After all, I'm only sixteen
Friends are friends until they're not
One day they're cold and next they're hot
Keep pretending to be someone you're not.

I really thought I liked you, a lot.

A Quiet Retreat

I can't stand the silence
Inside this empty house
I can almost see my breath
From when life was living here.

I can feel the echoes
Inside of my chest
Hallow where my soul was
Only now, there's nothing.

I can feel the tears
Swelling up inside
Begging to burst
With a single collide.

I am a balloon
Floating around the rooms
Nothing more than a ghost
A memory fading in thin air.

I wished for days that it would rain
So that maybe I'd be washed away
My body would float the streets
Passing through the people it meets.

IT CRESCENDOS

I'd float all the way to your step
With the little energy I have left
And ring your bell
Wishing you a final farewell.

Because no goodbyes were given
Just a closing of the door
Forced to move ahead
Like I've done *(a time or two)* before.

For now, I'll sit in silence
And wait for it to come
My body an avalanche
Waiting for the mountains to succumb.

One by one they will crumble
Piece by little piece
I too, will crumble
It's easier than a quiet retreat.

Head Games

Say my name
Say it out loud
I'm in my head
Where it's too loud.

Can't shut it up
I'll only shut you out
Can't see past this
Someone let me out.

I'm knock, knock, knocking
On my brain
Can't win these head games
Trapped inside my brain.

The words are there
On the tip of my lips
But there's a space there
And I might slip.

Roll the dice
It's your turn
I'm losing again
Stuck inside my head.

Chasing Rabbits

I woke up feeling confused today
I woke up feeling sad
I woke up with pictures in my head
Ones I wished I'd never had.

I woke up feeling lost
Even though I was home
Tears escaped my eyes
I hate feeling alone.

I woke up feeling fearful
Afraid I wouldn't forget
The hands you laid on me
Do you have any regrets?

I woke up feeling confused today
I woke up feeling bad
I woke up with pictures in my head
Ones I wished I'd never had.

I woke up feeling tired
I've forgotten how to sleep
I toss and turn, all night long
I dream and dream and dream.

Melody

I dream things that don't make sense
And then I dreamed of you
You were climbing high, too high
Until you fell inside a shoe.

The time on the clock
Does not move
My heart beats fast
Wishing time would pass.

Like Alice in Wonderland
Tumbling down the hole
Wondering where the poor Rabbit's gone
Something is terribly wrong.

That's when I wake
With a violent shake
I have been dreaming again
No time to say hello, my dear,
I'm running very late.

Paper Cut

A paper cut is all it was
The smallest slice
No harm done.

A straight line
Drawn in the sand
No trace of blood
Seen on my hand.

The pain is small
Yet significant to me
The rush of sting
Comes all too soon.

It's strange because
It's something only I can feel
Only time will heal
Even the smallest of cuts.

That's how grief can be too
Nobody sees the pain but you
Blurring my vision
Need a new prescription.

People keep moving
Night and day don't end
It passes by
Forgetting the eyes that have cried.

They say *you're not alone*
But aren't willing to
Pick up their phone
Because to them it's just a paper cut.

A scratch on their tiny surface
Is not my reality
The cut goes much deeper
As I watch myself bleed.

Pick up the pieces
Tend to my wound
Friends are just a Band-Aid
Covering up a bruise.

But today that'll be enough
To decide I'll be okay
Because everybody knows
That a paper cut never lasts forever,
Anyway.

Harmony

(hahr-muh-nee)

WHEN THE CHORDS AND PITCH ARE IN AGREEMENT

Knowing

I jumped into the boat
Without any oars
Praying we'd stay afloat
Believing we could coast.

Little did I know,
Which way the wind blows
It blew in every direction
I was supposed to know.

When the boat tipped over
We fell out
I thought for a moment we'd drown
Until an angel pulled us out.

That's when I saw a clearing
The sky opened wide
The clouds cracked and rain poured
We were safe and sound.

The waves roared alive
And brought us back to shore
Our good God has provided
For us, once more.

IT CRESCENDOS

The journey has been long
And it took a while to get there
But when we reached the shore
God had more in store.

I pulled out the map
The one God had given us
I opened it up and dived right in
This time He taught me how to swim.

He opened my eyes to the unknown
Led my heart where it was supposed to go
Little did I know
I wasn't meant to float on my own.

Freshman

The year you found out who your friends are
The year you drove your first car
The year you finally chewed gum in class
The year you swore you'd never pass.

The year you made up with your best friend
The year you rocked a brand-new trend
The year you discovered who you should be
The year you've been waiting for *finally.*

The year you feared the senior pranks
All the memories that this year creates
The year you said you'd never forget
Freshman year, live it with no regrets.

CLASS OF
2010

Long Way Home

I'm taking the long way home
Because I don't want to face the night alone
Lying in bed, staring at my phone
Thinking about you.

The songs are still playing in my head
The words you said, how could I forget?
Your smile, your laugh, your favorite hat
I'm reminded of you.

We took the long way home
As I stared out my window
Sitting quietly while you sang
My heart pounding loudly in my chest.

Words trapped inside
I had to swallow them down
And when I was alone, I cried
Because we always want what we can't have.

You may never be mine to hold
I may always be silver, while you're solid gold
Jealousy is the enemy
One of the bitter sides to me.

Harmony

Every time that I'm with you
I wish that I could kiss you
But the whole wide world would shake
And it would be my biggest mistake.

I'm torn between how I feel inside
I wish that I could call you mine
Even though I know this isn't right
I can't see past that night.

I'll slowly let you slip away
Erase you from my brain today
I won't reply to your texts anymore
It's about time I've closed this door.

Whenever I think about you
I'll remind myself that you're with her
I'll do my best to put on a happy face
Because it's the least that I can do.

When I feel alone at night
I'll just close my eyes real tight
Remind myself I'll be alright
Because we both know that I will.

I won't call you up when I feel scared
I won't show up at your door unaware
I won't say goodbye this time
I don't think that I could if I tried.

So, I'll take the long way home
Erase the words to this song
Because we used to hum along
But not this time.

I can't go back in time
There is no such thing as rewind
Don't worry about me
I'll be doing *just fine*.

I'm sorry if I led you on
I'm sorry if I was in the wrong
I really thought we might have a shot
Thought I learned my lesson but guess not.

These words might never leave this page
Words I don't have the courage to say
Because I know that they might hurt you
To know that I've been feeling this way.

I'll quietly go as I slip off these pages
I won't make a sound
The volume has been muted
I'll let you go as I take the long way home.

Rage

Inside of this
F-o-u-r- lettered room
Rage painted on the ceiling
The fan in the room
Doesn't do any good.

Inside of this
Broken celled cage
Rage in the shadows
Fear behind the windows
What's happened here?

It comes alive at midnight
And doesn't leave until noon
Somehow it lingers
Inside the small cracks
Don't look back.

Inside of this
Place like hell
Demons haunt you
You're under their spell
Too far gone now.

Inside of this
F-o-u-r lettered room
Rage painted on the ceiling
The fan in the room
Doesn't do any good.

Inside of this
Broken celled cage
Rage in the shadows
Fear behind the windows
Inside of this
Tiny little room called rage.

Cobwebs in My Mind

There are places you don't go
People you don't know
Lies you once believed
Webs you used to weave.

It's the you that you don't know
The faded memories
The broken reveries
The hidden parts of me.

They're the thoughts come creeping in
The nightmares that never end
The loss of a friend
A love that couldn't mend.

I've got cobwebs in my mind
I worry all the time
Of running out of time
Crossing over lines that aren't mine.

These cobwebs in my brain
Make me feel insane
The words I'll never say
A broken record on replay.

Quarantined

Here I am again
All these sleepless nights
There's a war inside my brain.

As I toss and turn
I let these feelings burn
Igniting the flame within.

Keep my thoughts at bay
Watch the words I say
Careful as I play.

Don't get too close
Is not what I fear the most
It's all the space between the lines.

I'll try and reach out to you
But you're far away
I will never forget another day.

I'll cherish those moments
I'll keep them safe
Even if they're only in my mind.

But that's just the thing
Eventually memories fade
Tomorrow presents another day.

Another day of holding on
And holding back
Of letting go and moving forward.

Forward motion
Two steps back
Can anyone still see me,
Through all these cracks?

Please don't let me slip away
To become nothing but a whisper
Gone with the wind.

Just a simple phone call away
So many things that I long to say
Someday, when we all meet again.

Love Me for Me

In the bottom of the well
Daydreaming about my future prince
But I'd never tell.

I remember chasing rainbows
Trying to find the pot of gold
The truth was hidden from me
Little did I know.

That when I stopped looking
Someday he would find me
And love me just the way I am.

I remember closing my eyes
Hoping to finally meet him
One day my prince will come.

I remember all the nights I cried
My young heart longing for "the one"
But only God held that key
Little did I know.

That when I stopped looking
Someday he would find me
And love me just the way I am.

Harmony

I remember the day I called off the search
My true love was finally found
I held onto hope, at the end of my rope
And he accepted me with open arms.

I'll never forget his smile
Genuine and pure
Little did I have to give,
Now my love is spilling over.

The day I stopped searching
He stopped searching too
He would love so effortlessly
All the pieces of me I failed to see.

I remember his hands, his lips
Our very first kiss
Our laughs and tickle fights
Long walks and late talks.

Call off the search
We have been found
Two broken people
Broken together, safe and sound.

Confessions

Confession
Sometimes I want to crawl inside a hole
Escape inside the darkness, erase my soul.
Confession
These are the deepest feelings that I hide
You can look but you won't find
Sometimes these confessions I keep inside.
Confession
Sometimes I drown myself in water
Taking in more than I can drink
I pretend I am an anchor that could sink.
Confession
I often feel empty rather than alive
I bleed on the outside, but don't wish to die
Sometimes these confessions I keep inside.
These are a few confessions of mine.

Midnight Whispers

I closed my eyes
It didn't
                    work
I heard a sound
My head
It   jerks
I climbed
Way out
Of my bed

          And strained my ears
          So that I could hear
          This little voice
                    ringing
                    inside
                    my head.

I couldn't hear
A single
          sound
The voice was
                    hushed

And my heavy heart
Inside my chest
          thumped,
          thumped,
          thumped.

IT CRESCENDOS

For a moment
I wasn't sure
That the

        thumping

                was even mine.

Lost with time
And the lonely

          midnight whispers.

Embers

There are words inside there
Trapped inside the barrel of my throat
Can't find their way out
The words stay hidden underneath.

All this anger
Roars like a lion
It shows its pearly teeth
Ready to pierce what's in between.

I can feel its claws
Digging one by one
But there are no lights here
The candles are blown out.

Close my eyes
Say a prayer
That sleep might meet my eyes
But it wears an ugly disguise.

A mask I painted delicately
Each line crafted perfectly
Only I see the cracks that might break
No room to make mistakes.

IT CRESCENDOS

Time doesn't exist
There are things I can't resist
I don't how to quit
Instead, I throw a fit.

It comes and goes as she pleases
Stealthy like a fox on her knees
The fox in my brain doesn't speak
She only knows how to steal and sneak.

I can feel the quiet of the house
My thoughts are terrifyingly loud
Cold beneath these sheets
That tangle me up with the secrets I keep.

The embers glow inside the kitchen
Or maybe it's from the living room
I don't know which room I'm in
My body is numb on the floor.

I catch a tiny piece of ash
Falling from the ceiling slow and fast
I didn't bother writing you a letter
Because I was never meant to stay.

Forget Me, Forget Me Not

I tied his necklace around my neck
Memories I tried to erase I started to recollect
I hung it from the doorknob
But I didn't choke, the necklace broke.

Surrendered on the floor
I was a tear-struck mess
Tears I had held in
I must confess.

I wish I could blow away
Like a dandelion in the wind
Like a small child
Carefree in the summer breeze.

I'd vanish in coffee made black
Like a dream before you wake up
Days that come and go
Season and birthdays,
People you used to know.

I wish sometimes I could just go
Go where the wind blows
A trail of lost love letters
A message in a bottle
Where buried treasures lie.

Sometimes I wish I could fall
Like someone falls out of love
When you fall out of line
Like when you stopped being mine.

It's kind of funny that I am here
Stuck in a reverie
Trying to chase away the memories
So, that one day maybe I won't have to remember,

All these terrible things
I wish so badly to forget.

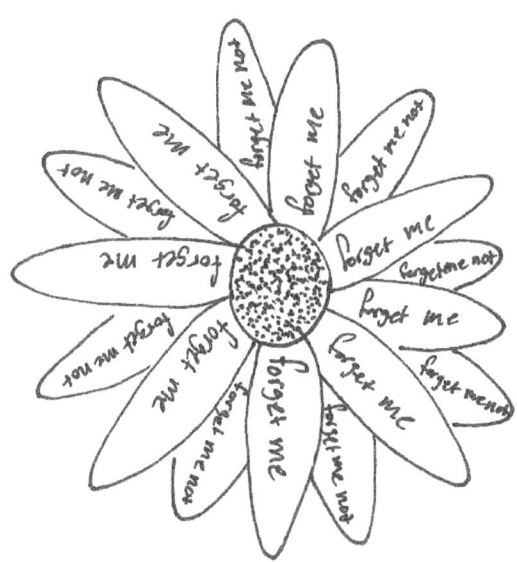

Bad-Hair Attitude

I'm a tangled mess
Black brush running through my hair
I'm a little distressed
My head is a rat's nest.

I try to straighten out the mess
All the kinks and places I might have missed
Can you tell, I'm a little obsessed?
And my hair is still a mess.

Nothing seems to work
I'm probably going to be late for work
My iron isn't hot enough
And I don't think I can call a bluff.

Part of me is calm, the other part is upset
So, for now, I'll put my hair up, up, up
Up into a ponytail
It's the least I can do, *for myself and for you.*

I think I need a new brush
It just isn't cutting it
But I can't seem to give it up
Even though my hair is wrecked.

There's a bunch of loose ends
Split ends and dead ends
Do you see what I'm getting at?
Are we still talking about hair?

This is where I fell apart
I've got this band too tight on my heart
There's only so much left I can do
If only I had a clue.

I woke up today a tangled mess
I'm overwhelmed and I'm stressed
I'm barely dressed; you're not impressed
With my bad-hair attitude.

Jenny

There are some things I need to say
But the words stick like chewing gum
Always getting in the way
Of the things I need to say.

It's okay to be different
Because that we truly are
Is it possible for our differences,
To have a heart-to-heart?

We're like two peas in a pod
Only it's not black and white
You're hot and I'm cold
I'm quiet and you're bold.

I don't know what to do
I don't like it when we fight
When we don't say the things, we should
I'm left wishing that you would.

What I'm really trying to say
Is that I miss you
Please believe that I still care
This silence is awkward, I'm aware.

I can't count the times
I've picked up my phone
Ready to call your number
Just like I've done a hundred times.

We've been friends *(the best ones)*
Throughout the years
Maybe it's about time
We finally shed a few tears *(I'm sorry)*.

When I say it's not you *(it's me)*
I'm telling you the truth
You're just expressing yourself
I shouldn't expect anything else.

There are some words I need to say
But the words linger on my tongue
Just know what I'd still do for you
I hope you'll forgive me, really, I do.

Sleepless Nights

Sleepless nights, this life
One moment you're high
The next you're burning down
But we learn
Pick ourselves up again
Promise not to do it again
What are we still doing here?
Does anybody make it out alive?

The pills, the sex
Do we do it for the thrill of it?
The rush, is it enough?
When it's just the two of us
The truth is we're dead inside
A ghost that's come to life
But are we *really* alive?

Can you forgive me
For the way I've been lately?
I'm not myself
I like to play pretend
Love hurts, but I like it that way
There's a lost girl somewhere inside
She plays pretend
Because it's easier to hide.

IT CRESCENDOS

Long nights, strange men
Looks like I'm at it again
I can't cope
With myself
All these sleepless nights
You left me bone dry
Did you think I'd never wonder why?
Did you think I'd be all right?

Sleepless nights, let's not fight
Tuck in the kids, I'll be just fine
Say my prayers, Lord, I need them
I need a sanctuary,
A safe place to rest my head
Because I can't escape
These nightmares in my bed.

The Words

I wish that I could write something
But I'm at a loss for words
I wish that I could say something meaningful
Like sunshine on a cloudy day
The words are somewhere, hibernating
Underneath my fingertips
I can feel the words breathing, pulsing, longing
But I can't usher them out.

I wish that I could write you
The words that you write for me
But the words don't come
They are somewhere hidden that I can't see
The page remains blank
What is it that I'm trying to say?
Am I letting myself get in the way?

My words are speechless
Quiet as a mumble
Softer than the drop of a pen
The ink is forever silenced
Not even eternity could set the words free
Am I writing for you?
Or am I writing for me?

IT CRESCENDOS

And then finally, in a single moment
The pen breathes and comes to life
As you draw your final breath
It is then, that I find my words at last.

Just One More

Just one more, says the loud voice I can't ignore
Slam the door, goodbye, I'm leaving.
Back for more, but I swear this will be my last.

Until I'm whole again, I won't return.

My heart aches with such a burden
I can't numb the thoughts inside my mind
Instead, I drown the memories I've left behind.

Erase myself— one drink later
I'll have *just one more* then I'll pay the tab
Catch a cab and then head home.

Home is where your bed is
But mine is empty without you by my side
I'll call you over
And I'll drink *just one more*
Because I know you'll be gone when I wake,
And I'll find myself staring at the door.

I'm slowly

D
    R
        I
            F
                T
                    I
                        N
                            G

My face is *numb*.

Just a shallow, hollow form of the person
I have become.
I'm okay here, really—I'll be fine, come tomorrow.

Another day, another drink
Who's to say I'm just wasting away?
I'll get better wait and see
I promise this one will be my last
You won't even recognize the new me.

Cheers to the fears
Nights drowning in tears
And lovers worth the pain
Raise your fist and I'll raise my glass,
Because tonight will be our last, I swear.

Brave like Lions

It is times like this
When I miss you most
Nights like this
When I want to hold you close.

The nights seem long
Without you by my side
Because when you're gone
Sadness comes to life.

Like a lion's roar
That I can't ignore
A burning inside my chest
I cannot put to rest.

It is times like this
I need to feel your warmth
Nights like this
That I long for your sweet kiss.

Lips locked, our hearts on fire
Can't put out this flame
We are only burning brighter
Our love will burn the city down.

IT CRESCENDOS

It is times like this
I can still breathe you in
It is strong and it is familiar
It is us together on a Tuesday.

The nights seem forever
Without you by my side
Because when you're not here
The sadness comes to life.

Like a lion's roar
That I can't ignore
A burning inside my chest
I cannot put to rest.

When I close my eyes
I can see your face
The waters are calm
I am not afraid.

No matter how far away
You may be
You are forever etched
Into my memory.

You are everything I want
And everything I need
You are the air in the morning
You are the best parts of me.

Harmony

My love is like a hurricane
I am the ocean, I am the rain
I am tomorrow and yesterday
Brave like lions, but our love cannot be tamed.

My Sonshine *(For you, Nana)*

I cannot see the sunshine today
It seemed like you were here just yesterday
I can see your smile
Can we stay here for a while?

I'd give anything just to see you
Embrace you like I used to
Every time I'd see you
But it wasn't enough.

I'm left with broken pieces
And old photographs
Trying my best just to remember
The sound of your laugh.

You were full of peace, joy, love, and warmth
You had a fire deep inside
That couldn't be contained
You were my *Sonshine* on my darkest days.

Jesus was the light inside your storm
He was your strength when you were tired and worn
You kept the light alive until the end
And now you're walking with Jesus, hand-in-hand.

Even if the sun does not shine
I will keep the light inside this heart of mine
And pray that through the clouds
He would open my eyes.

To see the beautiful *Sonshine*
That you're walking in right now
Letting go isn't ever easy
But I have a peace within somehow.

Our days may be dark ahead
But I know this is not the end
I cannot wait for the day I see you again
And forever we will be in His glorious *Sonshine.*

Sleeptalking

Are they cutting down trees?
He whispered to me
Eyes closed, half asleep.
No love, just go back to sleep
You must have been sleeptalking
It was just a silly dream.

My Black Oblivion

I'm three floors beneath
My two feet
The pages are torn
Ripped at the seams
I'm three floors too deep
I can't keep
Breathing, only sinking.

I'm three floors further
Then I was before
Nowhere to hide
Nowhere to go
I don't even know
The dark places I go
Three floors to nowhere
I don't know.

Falling into blackness
Getting there fast
Time doesn't exist
I feel my lungs collapse
I can't hold on
Everything is out of my reach
I won't hit rock bottom
Nothing is underneath
It's my black oblivion
I'll keep drowning if I speak.

Anxious Thoughts

I feel it first in my fingertips
And then it creeps up to my face
The heat quickly rises
From somewhere underneath.

Is it too soon to walk away?
Would they notice if I leave?
What a strange thing
This silly thing, tugging at me--*anxiety.*

I try and make small talk
Tiny words escape my lips
Like a door barely cracked enough
Won't let any light in.

The room is big, but I feel it closing in
My feet are grounded
My body still, yet I'm surrounded
By laughter and chatter
I'm not sure what's the matter, but I've got to go.

Fear is now gripping me
But I can't seem to leave
The party isn't over
I'm welcome here, come on over here
No thanks, I'm fine in my corner.

I know you, but I don't.
I don't know what to say
Conversation doesn't come easy
Don't worry, I've always been this way.

It's really not you, it's me
I don't know how to cure this disease
I don't have anywhere else to go
But my whole being would rather be home.

I need to go now
I've outgrown my stay
I don't have the words or warmth
We can catch up another day.

I've stayed longer than I planned for
In my mind I'm already out the door
And if I didn't care about being polite
I would have never come at all.

I'm starting to shrink in size
Like Alice under a spell
If I keep standing here
I might disappear as well.

Your home has been warm and inviting
I know I've said this before
Thank you very much
But really, I must go.

IT CRESCENDOS

We are the first to leave
And when the cold wind hits my face
I feel a weight letting go of me
Ahhh— I can finally breathe.

I feel the red in my cheeks
Slowly begin to fade
There's a sad bit in my heart
You see, all because of this stupid trick
And her name is Anxiety.

The Letter "M"

Monday mornings are for monkeys
Milkshakes are for Moms
Monsters munch M&Ms at the movies
Don't tell me that I'm wrong
Music makes me move
Mistakes make me mind my manners
Mundane is for the monks
Moose wear mittens
Mean girls don't move mountains
And *yes please,* to mac and cheese
Mmhmm please.

January

Quiet as a deer
In the falling snow
Winter is here
Watch the air escape your lungs
In a gentle glow
Laughter of children
Magic in the air
Wrapped in layers,
But I never feel prepared
For another season
Another reason
To bring in the new year---January.

ACKNOWLEDGMENTS

Now, for the trickiest part of the whole gig---appropriately expressing my genuine gratitude to all of those who have supported and cheered me on along this crazy ride (I hope you know who you are and how much I appreciate all that you've done for me, but here's a little THANKS in case you might have forgotten)!

My list of "thank you's" follows no order, simply wanted to thank you all from the bottom of my heart for being a part in this dream of mine that has finally come to life. First, I want to say thanks to my *love*, my FOREVERMATE, my lifelong partner, **Phil Starkey**. Thank you from the bottom of my heart all the way back to the tip-top, for all your love and support and, of course, late-night ramblings (because you and I both know there were many, many, nights of those!). Thank you for cheering me on and urging me to keep going on the nights I was near tears from all the stress of making it happen. You didn't give up the fight even when I was about to wave my flag. I love you!

Dearest friend, **Veronica**. I have poured out so many poems into your lap, that it's probably not even funny at this point! Or maybe it is a bit comical because I shared them with you whether or not you wanted to hear them. But no matter the occasion, you always seemed to receive my heart well and always got right to the matter of what my heart might have been trying to convey in that moment. Thank you for always listening and being that shoulder I could truly lean on.

Thank you, **Mr. Henderson**! I realize that you have a first name, but to me you will forever be Mr. Henderson. I have always looked up to you as a student, and now as an adult and writer myself, I admire your works and dedication to the writing process in its entirety. I wouldn't have made it this far if it hadn't been for you taking the time to try and answer all my questions. SO MANY QUESTIONS!! Also, a **BIG FAT** thanks for all the trouble you went through to make my book turn into a <u>real</u> book, *seriously* forever grateful!

Taylor Phillips! Huge shoutout to the gal that knows it all (well, most things!). I was amazed the moment I reached out to you with my curiosity to fully embrace this crazy world of self-publishing. You were so completely cool, calm, and collected--- exactly the fresh breath of air I needed amidst all the chaos running through my brain at the time! I don't know if I've ever "met" anyone as patient as you have been with me and all my questions. Even when you didn't have the answers, you always took the time to walk me through the pieces you did know, unapologetically. Thanks for guiding me through the valleys so that I could climb my way up to the mountaintop. I owe ya one!

Mikel: Of course, I'd include you in here too, gal! Even though our time working together on this collection was cut short, I am so thankful for the time that we did have together to collaborate, share our ideas and visions, and hit the ground running in each of our poetry endeavors! I sincerely wish you the best in your self-publishing journey and cannot wait to see your final masterpiece. Thanks again for all our late-night texts and poetry-talk!

Teresa! You didn't know your name would show up here, did you? Surprise! Thank you for letting me be a secret printer fairy in your office *(shh!)*. Don't worry, I don't think I made even the slightest dent in your ink cartridge, but if you twist my arm... I will gladly send you a free copy! (;

Mom and Dad: Thank you, thank you, a million times over, *thank you.* (**Branson,** you can be included in here too!) How can I ever thank you enough? Thank you for your unconditional love and support no matter how big or small my dream to write this book may have been. You saw me through from start to finish! You have never hesitated to be there rooting for me, cheering me on, and encouraging me to keep going even on the hardest of days. Thank you for inspiring me and my writing, I couldn't have come this far without your love and support.

Dad... even though I'm a writer, when it comes to giving you the amount of thanks you deserve, I know I'm going to come up short every time! You have done *so many* amazing things to ignite this dream-come-true that I don't even know where to properly begin. You are so much more than just the "behind the scenes." You're the above and beyond and all the little spaces in between. You knew exactly how to work your Photoshop magic and make this book everything I've ever dreamed of and more! You never hesitated with any part of the process and showed me grace in the messier parts of this journey. I love you to the moon and back and couldn't have done this bit without you!

BIG Thanks to my **family and friends**, you have all played such an important part as well! It might seem like you were just standing on the sidelines but the sidelines *matter!* You got the earliest, unscripted, rawest pieces of my poetry. I simply wrote it and shared some of my most vulnerable words with you. When I felt too afraid or naked to share it with anyone else, I shared it with you. Thank you for taking the time to receive my vulnerability in all my flaws and honesty and love me regardless. Thank you for being there then and thank you for being a part of my writing journey in the present.

MY NUMBER ONE THANKS GOES TO MY NUMBER ONE FAN, my Savior, Life Giver, constant cheerleader, and ultimate healer and restorer throughout my darkest days--- **Jesus Christ.** Thank you for allowing me to find your light when I was surrounded by darkness. Thank you for pouring yourself into me, so that one day I could pour myself into those that I am called to love. Thank you for blessing me with this beautiful opportunity to share a part of my story with the world. Your love crescendos, as does mine.

NOTES

Leonard, H. (1993). A cappella. *Pocket Music Dictionary* (pp. 8). Hal Leonard Publishing Corporation.

Leonard, H. (1993). Ballad. *Pocket Music Dictionary* (pp. 17). Hal Leonard Publishing Corporation.

Leonard, H. (1993). Crescendo. *Pocket Music Dictionary* (pp. 37). Hal Leonard Publishing Corporation.

Leonard, H. (1993). Harmony. *Pocket Music Dictionary* (pp. 60). Hal Leonard Publishing Corporation.

Leonard, H. (1993). Melody. *Pocket Music Dictionary* (pp. 75). Hal Leonard Publishing Corporation.

Index

A Catch in the Wind	105
A Quiet Retreat	177
A Stranger's Secret	112
Amazing	47
Anxious Thoughts	224
Astronauts	58
Aurora	86
Bad-Hair Attitude	207
Before the Storm	51
Blue Jeans	40
Blue Skies	45
Brave	55
Brave like Lions	217
Bruises	63
Chasing Rabbits	180
Chocolate Milk	24
Cinnamon	167
Cobwebs in My Mind	195
Confessions	200
Embers	203
Falling for You	163
For My Dad	13
For My Mom	15
Forbidden Love	141
Forevermore	29
Forget Me, Forget Me Not	205
Freshman	189

Friend	85
Going Home	136
Goodbyes are Harder than I Thought	129
Green-Eyed Girl	150
Happily, Ever After, It's Not the End	32
Happy Birthday	44
Head Games	179
High School Drama Queen	175
Hilltop Bruises	20
Home	74
I Am	65
I Can Play with Fire Too	153
I Wrestled a Bear	62
In Loving Memory	125
It Crescendos	7
January	228
Jenny	209
Just a Dream	12
Just One More	215
Just Us Kids	54
Ka-Boom	53
Knowing	187
Long Way Home	190
Love Me for Me	198
Love You So	38
May Fever	91
Midnight Whispers	201
My Black Oblivion	223

My Reflection   37
My Sonshine   220
New Beginnings   11
Nothing   43
One of Those Girls   142
Our Sky is Everybody's Sky   42
Paper Cut   182
Phoebe   28
Places I've Been   127
Powerless Words That Have the Spark to Ignite   17
Quarantined   196
Rage   193
Raindrops   101
Remembrances of Me   160
Rescue Me   161
Restart Button   27
Rose   171
Roxy   138
Running in Place   122
Sleepless Nights   211
Sleeptalking   222
Solid Ground   79
Speechless   67
Still Inspired   148
The Anchor   133
The Angst of Breaking Up   143
The Canvas   104
The Garden   66
The Grand Opening   115

The Great Gatsby	97
The Highs and Lows	156
The Island	131
The Key	146
The Letter "M"	227
The Mountaintop	165
The Orange Tree	110
The Promise	169
The Prophylactic Drug	95
The Sun Will Never Rise	71
The TV	34
The Waiting Post	99
The Words	213
The Wreckage	87
Things I Never Said	18
Tiptoe	158
Tomorrow	69
Toxic	172
Turn on the Lights, Monsters are out Tonight	76
Unseen	118
Until We Meet Again	60
Where Did I Go?	73
While I Wait	22
White	82
Without You (Alone)	107
Yesterday	93
You're the One	83

Photo Credit: SD Photography 2022

Delon Nicole Starkey was born in Dallas, TX but considers herself an Oklahoma gal at heart. She was an Okie native from 2005-2022. She graduated NWOSU with her master's degree in professional counseling. She currently lives in Ohio with her husband and two kids. She enjoys drinking coffee any time of the day and long summer days in the sunshine. She's a mom, writer, blogger, and lifelong Jesus follower.

Instagram: @starkey.delon
Word Press: girlimcomingover.wordpress.com

Anthony Coursey has loved illustrating from a young age; it is something that has always come effortlessly to him, and he does so with passion and ease. His love for drawing has continued to grow over the years. And his artistic ability doesn't stop with pen and paper either, he has designed tattoo artwork, custom light switches, business logos, and even holiday cards and banners for special events. Born and raised in Northwest Oklahoma, Anthony still resides there and enjoys spending his free time with his beautiful wife and their two young children.

Facebook: Coursey Custom Art

www.ingramcontent.com/pod-product-compliance
Lightning Source LLC
Chambersburg PA
CBHW071151130626
46553CB00004B/1614